3 SECRETS TO THE HAPPY AND HEALTHY RELATIONSHIP YOU'VE ALWAYS F*CKING WANTED

WENDY MILLER

CONTENTS

Preface — ix

Introduction — xiii

Secret #1 — Food — 1

Fun Food Facts 1 — 2

Sandwiches — 3

Sloppy Joe Grilled Cheese — 4

Patty Melt with Brie Cheese and Caramelized Onions — 6

Fun Food Facts 2 — 9

Tuna Avocado Melt — 10

The Easiest Reuben Sandwich — 12

Grilled Cheese Sandwich With Extra Love — 14

Melty Roast Beef Sandwich — 16

Fun Food Facts 3 — 18

Slow Cooker Recipes — 19

Idiot-Proof Slow Cooker BBQ Ribs — 20

Chile Colorado — 22

Slow Cooker Turkey Chili — 24

Slow Cooker Shredded Chicken Teriyaki — 26

You Barely Have to Care Barbeque Pulled Pork Sandwiches — 28

Simply Shredded French Dip — 30

Super Sexy Slow Salsa Chicken — 32

Fun Food Facts 4 — 34

Pasta — 35

Cheesy Chili Mac — 36

One-Pot Pasta Miracle — 38

One-Pot Half-Hour Creamy Tomato Basil Pasta Bake — 40

Super Sexy Creamy Mac and Cheese — 42

Simple Homemade Lasagna — 44

Linguini with Shrimp and Spinach — 46

Cavatelli and Broccoli — 48

Meat — 50

Salt and Pepper Skirt Steak — 51

Perfect Pork Chops	52
Melty Mozzarella Stuffed Barbeque Meatloaf	54
Perfect Pan-Seared Steak	56
The Easiest, Fastest Swedish Meatballs Ever	58
Steak Kabobs	60
Grandma's Beef Stew	62
Fun Food Facts 5	64
Poultry	65
Lemon Grilled Chicken Breasts	66
Grilled Chicken and Zucchini Kabobs	68
Sheet Pan Chicken with Sweet Potatoes and Brussels Sprouts	70
Easy Breezy Chicken Tacos	72
No Jive Turkey Shepherd's Pie	74
Beyond-Easy Baked Turkey Meatballs	76
Hot and Sexy Fried Chicken Tenders	78
Fun Food Facts 6	80
Seafood	81
Seared Ahi Tuna Steaks	82
Super Fab Crab Cakes	84
Seared Salmon with Fresh Dill Sauce	86
Trampy Shrimp Scampi	88
One Cool Catfish	90
Fun Food Facts 7	92
Breakfast	93
Waffle Tots Epic Breakfast Sandwich	94
Cheesy Baked Eggs Over Grits	96
Spinach Breakfast Tacos	98
Gluten-Free Almond Meal Spinach and Mushroom Quiche	100
Breakfast Nachos	102
Dutch Dutch Baby	104
Desserts	107
Totes Yummy Banana Bread	108
Paleo Chocolate Chip Cookies	110
Super Simple Snacks	112
Fun Food Facts 8	115
Secret #2 — Sex	116
How To Tame A Wild Penis	117
Slooooooooooow Down	118
Lube 101	119

Befriend His Frenulum 123

Let His Boner Do the Talking 124

Mouthwatering 125

Can I Get a Show of Hands? 126

Get Deep 127

Love Can Be Blind 128

The Eyes Have It 129

The Taint of Heart 130

Go Nuts 132

On the Other Hand . . . 133

The Over and Over 134

Around the Cock 135

A New Twist 136

A Stroke of Genius 137

Hands Together Now 138

Pray a Big Part 139

Okay by Him 140

It's The Little Things 141

She's a Very Kinky Girl . . . 142

Confidence Can Get You Very Far 143

Consent 144

Do Ask, Do Tell 146

Sexytime Stuff! 148

Pearls 149

A Yoga Ball 150

Wax On, Get Off 151

Good Vibes All Around 152

Fit To Be Tied Up 154

The Secret Life of Scrunchies 155

Plastics! 156

Buzzzzzz-ang! 157

A Naughty Vault 158

Keep it Clean When You're Getting Dirty 159

Adventures 161

Visit Your Local Sex Shop 162

Get Some Class! 163

Motel Hell-o! 164

Naked Day! 166

Don't Do This, Whatever You Do 167

Room with a Screw 169

Roleplaying! 170

Be Around Other Naked People   171
Fun with Your Clothes On   173
Dirty Talk   174
Fuck Shui   176
Get a Damn Lock!   177
TV Is Your Friend   179
Turn Down the Lights   180
The Picture-Perfect Bedroom   182
Clutter Is a Boner Killer!   183
Sheet Music   184
Soundproofing   185
Secret #3 — Leave Him Alone   186
Are You Afraid of Something? Do It!   188
Sex With The Person You Love Most   190
Take Yourself to the Edge   192
Choose Your Words Wisely   194
Write a Thank-You Letter   198
Make Good on Your Promises   200
Interview an Old Person   202
Travel Back in Time   204
Take a Walk   206
Take a Community College Class   209
Test Drive Your Dream Car   211
Eat Some Damn Doughnuts   213
Take a Bicycle Tour   215
Strap On A Toolbelt   218
Clear Out Your Crap!   220
Clean Out Your Box   224
Pitch A Tent   226
Learn Tarot   230
Write a Song   232
Get Moving   233
Pet Project   235
Tell Yourself to Shut Up   237
Help Other Women   244
Learn From Other People's Mistakes   250
Afterword   255
Thank you   259
Acknowledgments   260
Sex Ed The Musical   262
About The Author   263

This book is dedicated to my practically perfect in every way husband, Karl T. Wright, the dreamiest, sweetest, and most patientest man in the history of men; and to my ridiculous parents, Joy and Leonard Miller, who have been happily married for sixty-five years and still speak to each other almost every day.

I also dedicate this book to tacos, 'cause I really love them, too.

PREFACE

It is a dilemma that has plagued women for hundreds of years. Fortunes have been spent on relationship and self-help manuals, classes, videos, magazines, counseling, airport hotel seminars, uncomfortable lingerie, scented body lotions, battery-operated devices, supplements, and perilously high heels, all by women hoping to figure out the secrets to a happy, lasting relationship.

Ladies, as your new best friend, I am here to tell you that just like almost everything else in your life, you are HUGELY over-thinking this thing.

We've all spent a fortune and read every damn thing out there, trying to figure out how to keep men happy when, in all honesty, there ain't much there to figure out. Because when it comes down to it, men are a) excellent at fitting lots of things into the trunk of a car; 2) a lot easier to please than you've ever over-thought; and iii) about as complex as a disposable fork. Maybe even less.

Strap in, because you are finally about to figure out this entire thing. However, I must warn you that my theory might be some-what difficult for some of you to grasp at first.

That's because it's so simple. There is a logical fallacy called Complexity Bias. When faced with two competing theories, we humans are wired to choose the more complex one and completely devalue anything simple. Noted Dutch theoretical physicist Edsger W. Dijkstra famously said, "Simplicity is a great virtue but it requires hard work to achieve it and education to appreciate it. And to make matters worse: complexity sells better."

Here's a perfect example. I was at a party for the parents at my daughter's school. There was music, booze, chocolate-dipped bacon — all of the things. I had just finished dancing with my husband and was heading to get some water when a group of moms called me over. Knowing my background, they were looking for some *specialized* advice. One of the moms asked, "We're not having very much sex with our husbands and it's starting to worry us. Are there some herbs or sex toys or some products you could recommend that will help us to feel more connected to them?" I looked at the three women huddled together and then looked all the way across the room and saw their husbands standing with each other. I said, "Well, if you want to feel more connected to your husbands, one thing you can do is start spending more quality time with them, ya know, like at this party?" The women looked across the room at their husbands and then back to me, and one said, "Aren't there just some herbs or some other things we can buy instead?

Now, I realize I'm not a licensed therapist, psychologist, guru, life coach, swami, shaman, or cable news pundit. However, I do bring a unique level of expertise to this world that no one else can match. As an ACS Certified Sexologist, I spent more than seven years as head of programming for Playboy TV, where I developed, created, and oversaw hundreds of hours of premium shows designed *specifically* for couples—network-quality TV programming created to inspire more openness and communication in order to increase intimacy and sexual pleasure for couples.

Based on a thorough research study of couples, *Playboy* discovered that the more couples talk about sex and share their desires with each other, the more sex and intimacy they have and the happier they are.

I created hundreds of hours of programming designed specifically to keep couples sexually in sync. Working with some of the world's leading sex educators and experts, I embedded myself, ovaries deep, in the world of human sexuality and desire. Becoming the Dian Fossey of swingers, I learned everything I could about advanced sexual techniques, acceptance, desire, freedom from judgment and shame, and the pursuit of true pleasure. My understanding of sex, communication, and pleasure evolved exponentially. The student became the master.

For years I've been hosting a popular weekly podcast called *Sex Ed The Musical* that has featured dozens of leading experts in the fields of pleasure, successful relationships, sex therapy, and self-care for women. Plus, I've been with my husband for thirty-two years, and I assure you, he is one happy guy.

It is my goal in life to improve the lives of other women by sharing my understanding of sex and what it takes to enjoy a successful, happy relationship. I've hosted sold-out advanced sexual technique seminars. I've sat among renowned physicians and sexuality experts on panels at women's events. I'm the Sexpert Next Door for my vanilla suburban friends. My life's work is to help women step away from the shame and judgment we've all been taught about sex, and to empower and support each other to own, honor, and enjoy our sexual desires.

Bona fides aside, no matter where I am or who I'm talking to, one question keeps coming up over and over and over again.

What's the Secret to a Happy and Healthy Relationship?

Okay. I'm about to hand you the keys to this kingdom. All I ask is that you give yourself space not to overthink this. Because just like men, my theory is impossibly simple.

Read this book, memorize it, start a book club for it. Buy multiple copies for your friends, and memorize every damn word I've written.

In the end, you will never be huddled together with your married girlfriends at a party wondering where it all went so horribly wrong. Oh, and you'll also have the Happy and Healthy Relationship You've Always Fucking Wanted.

Your dirty best friend and new favorite author,

Wendy Miller

INTRODUCTION

When I first started writing this book, the idea was so simple that I had planned for it to be only one page of text followed by 150 blank pages where you could track your progress, save your thoughts, journal about your hopes and dreams, or draw pornographic pictures of George Clooney. This plan wasn't entirely based on laziness. I know that my complete thesis can be explained in just one page, or even in a few seconds. It's that simple.

But then I started thinking about the value of going much deeper. After all, you could say that the theory of relativity is $E=mc^2$ and be done with it. But that takes all the fun out of physics. So I decided to share my theory, and also give women the tools they need to put it into play. I am here to inform and empower you, because women buy books with those keywords in them. Also, because everything I'm about to say is hella fucking true.

Now, some fellas might get a little butthurt by reading this book, and like most women, I have been socialized to be responsible for their feelings. Unfortunately for them, I have also been anti-socialized to give zero fucks about what men think.

Hey, get angry, guys. Get reeeeeeeeally angry. Complain! Talk about how much you hate this book all over social media everywhere. Don't forget Reddit. Go ahead, complain endlessly about this book. That will totally show me. Be sure to use hashtags.

Also, in case you didn't realize, this book is actually designed to keep you dummies happy. I only wrote it because I think you're cute, and I totally suck at getting lots of items into the trunk of my car. Not necessarily in that order.

Also, even though I'm not, you'll notice that this version of the book is heteronormative. I am both playing with and shaking up gender roles that can suck the magic out of heterosexual relationships, and that's not necessarily the kind of sucking we're all after, if you know what I mean. This book also centers relationships between cisgender women and cisgender men because in my life and work, this subset of the population has been the most likely to send out an S.O.S. around S.E.X.

As an ally to my queer and trans loved ones, it felt important to name that and to use this as a teaser for subsequent editions that will be tailored to support other gender identities, sexual orientations and relationship configurations. I love everybody as they are and I want my work to be as inclusive as possible. Plus, with the queer editions I know I'll have much more fabulous book readings. Sorry straights, but you know I'm right.

Hey, let's all win!

In this particular version, I'm talking to women who live with penis owners. I congratulate all of you for your commitment to trying to solve the age-old question: What's the secret to a happy, and healthy relationship?

Now please step away from any complexity bias and understand that despite what you think, have read, have seen on TV, or have overheard in the dressing room at TJ Maxx, it turns out that in order to enjoy a lifetime of love, you only have to do **THREE THINGS** (in no particular order, except probably #2 before the others). And the best part is, you don't have to do all three all the time. Mix it up. Keep your guy on his toes and be sure to take the most time for yourself. Because, do that.

Alright then, what are the three secrets to a happy and healthy relationship? I assure you, this is not rocket science. It's Relationship Strategy, which doesn't have as many nifty space logo patches but is actually responsible for a lot more happiness in this world.

Relationships are a dance, and unfortunately, we often have to let those dummies lead because that's what they've been taught to do for millennia in this stupid patriarchy. But WE ALL KNOW that women are in charge of every major decision that takes place in a typical male/female partnership.

Women make 80% of all purchasing decisions in the home. We control the purse strings, we control the parenting, we control food purchases. Otherwise, dudes would be stocking the cabinets with craft beer and cool ranch chips, then enjoying said bounty in their tattered underwear while sprawled out on a massive sectional sofa made out of autographed footballs.

We are the ones who handle every fucking thing around here. So as usual, we're about to handle them, too.

But since they are kind of fun, with my help, you'll get this locked down to the point where you OWN your dude. Like seriously own. He's happy. You're happy. A happy and healthy relationship follows.

HERE'S ALL YOU HAVE TO DO...

#1 Give Him Food. Whether it's a sandwich, pizza, or New York steak au poivre with a brandy cream sauce and haricots verts: Men Want Food. You can make this easy on yourself or difficult. In the following pages, I offer you fifty shockingly simple recipes that will that will melt your guy's heart with a paltry amount of effort from you.

#2 Give Him Sex. Whether it's fast, slow, kinky, vanilla, fully costumed, semi-participatory, or even when they're not fully awake: Men Want Sex. You can make it begrudging or fun. In the following pages, I have fifty sex techniques, adventures, and my favorite sexytime items that can make it totally fun for both of you.

#3 Leave Him Alone. This one may be the most challenging one for you to grasp, and I assure you it's nothing personal, but men frequently want to be left alone. Now, the first thing you need to understand is that this has nothing whatsoever to do with you. It's not a rejection, it's actually a perfect opportunity. They need to be in their stupid man worlds doing whatever stupid shit men do for hours at a time that you almost certainly wouldn't want to be part of anyway.

AND THAT'S THE GENIUS OF #3! This is the portion of the book, and therefore your life, where you don't have to think about those people and whatever they want.

1 and 2 will cover that perfectly.

Number 3 is all about YOU!

This is for you to do whatever the hell YOU want to do on YOUR own terms, while at the same time, he's getting the things he requires in order to be happy forever.

I'll say it again. This time in bold so you know I mean business.

Number 3 is all about YOU! Only you!

Look…if it will make you feel better, pretend you're all bummed out when you leave to do really fun things without him. He will never know you're secretly thrilled (a recurring theme within this book).

Plus, he really wants to be left alone to do whatever stupid shit he likes to do anyway, which, trust me, works out rather nicely for you.

SECRET #1 — FOOD

NOTHING SAYS "I LOVE YOU" LIKE SOMETHING COVERED IN MELTED CHEESE

Author's Note: Please remember, when preparing any of the following recipes, always make it appear as if you worked really hard on everything, when in actuality, these recipes are specifically designed for you to put in hardly any effort at all.

You'll also notice that I completely ignore the concept of serving sizes in these recipes. I do so because there's no such thing as an Official Serving Size. The serving sizes listed on Nutrition Facts labels are based on decades-old surveys conducted by the FDA. They're merely suggestions and not officially recommended serving sizes.

The entire serving size concept is a bullshit social construct. Maybe two Oreos is a serving size for someone out there, but sometimes an entire row of Oreos is the ideal serving size. There's nothing wrong with either one. So please don't look for serving sizes in any of these recipes.

Eat however damn much you want to eat, that's what I'm serving.

FUN FOOD FACTS 1

My trainer told me to eat the way I want to look.

So I'm having Beyoncé for lunch.

SANDWICHES

When I was in the early stages of researching this book, I decided to test my theory on the biggest knuckle-dragging dude I know, my very own brother, Darren. We were playing golf and he had just finished urinating on a poor, defenseless tree, as he does every time we play golf.

I explained that after years of exhaustive research, I realized that men really want only three things: a sandwich, a blowjob, and to be left alone. He considered what I said for a moment and then asked, "What kind of sandwich?"
It was at that point I knew I was onto something.

So in honor of my brother Darren, a man who never met a golf course he didn't pee on, or a meat sandwich he didn't like, I present you with…

SANDWICHES!

SLOPPY JOE GRILLED CHEESE

What dude wouldn't want a sandwich with a manly name? Especially a man who is defiantly unkempt. Double manly! This is one of my husband's favorite dinners, and you can use ground beef, ground turkey, plant-based meat, or even tofu, I suppose. I mean, I wouldn't, but you totally can.

Total Time :25 • Yield: 4 sandwiches

Ingredients

- 1 pound lean ground beef, ground turkey, plant-based meat, or tofu
- 1/2 medium onion, chopped
- 1/4 cup green pepper, chopped
- 2/3 cup ketchup
- 1 1/2 teaspoons Worcestershire sauce
- 1 teaspoon ground mustard
- 1/2 teaspoon garlic powder
- 1/8 teaspoon cayenne pepper
- 4 buns, because dudes like buns
- 1 cup cheddar cheese, shredded

Instructions

1. Brown ground beef or ground turkey in a nonstick pan placed over medium heat. If you're using plant-based meat or tofu, follow its cooking instructions. Use a wooden spoon to break the beef or turkey apart as it cooks. Once it's browned you could drain the fat but, really, why bother?

2. Add the onion and green pepper. Cook until the protein is no longer pink and onion and pepper are softened.

3. Add ketchup, dry mustard, garlic powder, Worcestershire sauce, and cayenne pepper. Stir to combine well and cook over medium-low heat for 5 minutes. Remove from heat.

4. Toast bun lightly. Top with sloppy joe mixture. Then top with cheese.

5. Watch happy guy devour sloppy joes.

PATTY MELT WITH BRIE CHEESE AND CARAMELIZED ONIONS

Oooooh, fancy! Okay, don't get all worried. This is basically a bougie patty melt that will look like you put in a lot of effort but really didn't. Ya'welcome.

Total Time :25 • Yield: 4 sammitches

Ingredients

- 1 pound ground beef or ground turkey
- 1 tablespoon Worcestershire sauce
- Salt
- Freshly ground black pepper
- 1/4 teaspoon onion powder
- 1/4 teaspoon garlic powder
- 1/4 teaspoon paprika
- Olive oil or canola oil
- 2 medium onions, halved and sliced thinly (semi-circles)
- 8–16 slices triple cream brie cheese (depending on size of bread)
- 8 slices sourdough bread, lightly buttered on one side

Instructions

1. Place the ground beef or turkey into a large bowl. Add the Worcestershire sauce, 1/2 teaspoon of salt, 1/4 teaspoon of freshly ground black pepper, onion powder, garlic powder, and paprika. Mix the seasoning thoroughly into the meat.
2. Divide the meat into 4 equal patties (4 ounces each) that will fit on your sourdough bread.
3. Once formed, place the patties on a plate, cover with plastic wrap, and set aside for 20 minutes to allow the seasoning to penetrate and flavor the meat. Hahaha, penetrate!
4. While the patties are getting consensually penetrated, place a large nonstick skillet over medium-high heat, and add in about 2 tablespoons of oil.
5. Add in the sliced onions plus a couple of pinches of salt and pepper, and caramelize the onions until a deep, golden brown—this takes about 10 minutes.
6. Spoon the onions into a bowl and cover to keep warm; set aside.
7. Place the same nonstick skillet back over medium-high heat. Add a drizzle of oil to the pan, and once hot, add two patties (or however many fit comfortably into the pan) and cook for a couple of moments on the first side; next, flip the patties over and cook a little longer, until cooked to your favorite temperature. Remove the patties onto a plate, and repeat the process with any remaining patties. Clean out the skillet.
8. To assemble the sandwiches, place 2–3 slices of brie cheese on the side of the bread that is not buttered, and over that, add about 1/4 of the caramelized onions. Next, add a patty, another 1–2 slices of cheese, and cover with another slice of bread with the buttered side up.
9. Once all sandwiches are assembled, place the skillet over medium-high heat and once hot, add a couple

sandwiches to the pan (buttered-side down), pressing down on them with a spatula or a bacon press to help everything melt together. Allow the sandwiches to become toasted and golden brown delicious on the first side. Once G.B.D., gently flip, pressing down again, and allow them to toast on the other side until the cheese is melty (cover the pan if necessary to help the cheese melt). Repeat the process with the remaining sandwiches.

10. Cut the sandwiches in half and serve while hot.
11. Watch happy guy destroy your fancy patty melt.

FUN FOOD FACTS 2

Everybody knows the Earl of Sandwich invented the sandwich. But very few people know he also invented potato chips, carrot sticks and fruit salad in disposable plastic cups.

TUNA AVOCADO MELT

This is my favorite sandwich of all time, and since I'm making dinner, we get what I want. See how that works? Everybody wins, and when I say everybody, I mean you.

Total Time :15 • Yield: 4 sangwiches

Ingredients

- 2 (5-ounce) cans of your favorite chunk light tuna, packed in water, drained
- 3 tablespoons mayonnaise
- 2 tablespoons butter
- 1 avocado, peeled, pitted, and sliced
- 4 slices Jack cheese
- 8 slices of your favorite bread

Instructions

1. Mix tuna with mayonnaise.
2. Butter one side of each slice of bread.
3. Heat nonstick skillet over medium heat.
4. Place 4 slices of bread, butter side down, in skillet.
5. Top bread with tuna/mayo mixture.
6. Layer 2–4 slices of avocado.
7. Place Jack cheese on top of avocado.
8. Top sandwich with other slice of bread, butter side facing up.
9. Once bottom of bread is golden brown delicious, flip to toast the other side.
10. The cheese will melt during the heating.
11. His heart will melt during the eating.

THE EASIEST REUBEN SANDWICH

I have a very close friend who had a big crush on Reuben Kincaid from *The Partridge Family*. He's dead now—the actor, not my friend. Although, I haven't called my friend in a while. I probably should. Anyway, it turns out, several people named Reuben claimed to have invented this sandwich. They're all dead now, too. Hopefully not from the sandwich.

Total Time :15 • Yield: 4 saniches

Ingredients

- 2 tablespoons butter, softened
- 8 slices rye bread
- 8 slices Swiss cheese
- 3/4 pound corned beef brisket, thinly sliced
- 1/2 pound sauerkraut
- 1/4 cup pre-made Russian dressing, because you've got too much shit to do to be making Russian dressing from scratch and he'll never know the difference anyway
- Pre-made coleslaw because it's totally fine

Instructions

1. Butter one side of four slices of bread and place the slices buttered side down on a large piece of wax paper on a flat surface. Top each with a slice of Swiss cheese, and then divide half of the corned beef among them.
2. Using paper towels, squeeze out excess moisture from the sauerkraut and divide among the sandwiches, and top each with one tablespoon of Russian dressing. Add another layer of corned beef and a second slice of Swiss cheese to each sandwich. Top with the remaining bread slices; butter the side facing out.
3. Preheat a griddle or frying pan to medium heat. Cook the sandwiches on one side until the bread is golden brown delicious. Use a spatula to carefully flip the sandwiches over and finish cooking on the second side. Cut the sandwiches in half before serving.
4. Serve with a side of coleslaw and serious attitude, knowing this sandwich rules.

GRILLED CHEESE SANDWICH WITH EXTRA LOVE

Even though basic grilled cheese sammies are not considered that difficult, adding perfectly crisp bacon and sliced tomatoes makes it seem as if you really care. Are you catching on yet? This recipe calls for cheddar cheese, but you can totally use American cheese. I do, however, strongly suggest you DO NOT use turkey bacon. *That* is a dream deferred.

Yes, I just quoted Langston Hughes in a grilled cheese sandwich recipe. You know why? 'Cause I was a fucking English major!

Total Time :20 • Yield: 4 sammies

Ingredients

- 8 slices bacon
- 1/4 cup butter, softened
- 8 slices of your favorite bread
- 8 slices cheddar cheese (or Uhmurrican)
- 8 thin slices tomato—remove that hard, yucky white part in the middle, no one wants that shit.

Instructions

1. Cook bacon until evenly brown and crispy. You can use a skillet, the microwave, or even the oven. Choices!
2. Heat a large skillet over medium heat.
3. Spread butter onto one side of each slice of bread.
4. Lay 4 slices of bread, butter side down, in the skillet.
5. Top with a slice of cheese, 2 slices of tomato, 2 pieces of bacon, and another slice of cheese.
6. Cover with a slice of bread, butter side out.
7. Cook sandwiches until golden brown delicious on both sides.
8. The sandwich is done when the cheese is melted.
9. Cut in half on a diagonal to show that you really care.
10. Pairs nicely with potato tots, a small green salad, and a handjob.

MELTY ROAST BEEF SANDWICH

In this recipe I use cooked roast beef from the local deli counter. You know why? 'Cause you ain't got time to make an entire roast for a sandwich. What are you, your mother?

Total Time :20 • Yield: 4 samijes

Ingredients

- 2 tablespoons olive oil
- 2 garlic cloves, minced
- 1/8 teaspoon crushed red pepper flakes
- 1/2 pound sliced deli roast beef
- 1/2 cup beef broth
- 2 tablespoons additional beef broth
- 2 teaspoons dried parsley flakes
- 2 teaspoons dried basil
- 1/4 teaspoon salt
- 1/4 teaspoon dried oregano
- 1/8 teaspoon pepper
- 4 sandwich rolls, split
- 4 slices provolone cheese

Instructions

1. In a large cast-iron skillet, heat oil over medium-high heat.
2. Add garlic and pepper flakes; cook and stir 1 minute.
3. Add roast beef, broth, and seasonings; heat through.
4. Place beef slices on rolls; drizzle with additional broth. Top with cheese.
5. Man + meat + cheese = HAPPY

FUN FOOD FACTS 3

In the mid 1970s, the slow cooker
was marketed as:

"Perfect for Working Women"

You know what would *really* be perfect
for working women?

Equal pay for doing the same fucking jobs
as working men!

SLOW COOKER RECIPES
SET IT, FORGET IT, TAKE ALL THE DAMN CREDIT!

You may be shocked to learn that this book has not been nominated for a James Beard Award. That's because they don't have a category for:

**Best Cookbook That Also Features
Advanced Handjob Techniques**.

At least they didn't the last time I checked.

Nevertheless, you should get a slow cooker. It's the easiest way to braise meats or cook up a huge pot of chili. In fact, I once used mine to decarboxylate some weed.

I'm like a naughty pioneer woman.

IDIOT-PROOF SLOW COOKER
BBQ RIBS

Imagine walking into a house where the smell of pork and barbeque sauce fills the air. Mmmm. That will be *your* house when you prepare this recipe. It's like magic.

Total Time 8:10 • Servings: You get to decide that, not me

Ingredients

- 1 rack baby back pork ribs
- 2 teaspoons chili powder (or chipotle chili powder if you prefer)
- 1 teaspoon garlic powder
- 1/2 teaspoon cayenne pepper
- 1/2 teaspoon salt
- 1/4 teaspoon pepper
- 2 cups of his favorite BBQ sauce because life is easier when you just get what he wants and it's already in a jar in Aisle 9

Instructions

1. Grease your large slow cooker (6–8 quart) with nonstick spray. Stir together chili powder, cayenne pepper, garlic powder, salt, and pepper. Rub mixture all over the top side of the ribs.
2. Brush about 2/3 of the BBQ sauce over the ribs (reserve remaining BBQ sauce), top and bottom. Place the ribs in the slow cooker so that they are standing up on one side and curl to fit around the inner edge of the slow cooker. Cover and cook on low for 8 hours.
3. Preheat your oven to broil. Use tongs to transfer ribs to a greased baking sheet so that the ribs are now lying flat. Place them in the oven and cook for 5–8 minutes. (Stay right there and check them to make sure they aren't burning.) Allow to cool just long enough so that the ribs can be handled and serve immediately.
4. Serve with a side of I-seriously-know-how-to-please-this-dude realness.

CHILE COLORADO

I've only been to Colorado once, and that's because my flight had to make an emergency landing in Denver. It was right out of a movie, except nothing interesting actually happened.

I'm sure Colorado is lovely.

Total Time 8:30 • Servings: You decide, I'm not judging you

Ingredients

- 1 teaspoon of olive or vegetable oil
- 1 small white onion, finely chopped
- 2 cloves garlic, minced
- 1/2 teaspoon cumin
- 1/2 teaspoon dried oregano
- 3 whole dried ancho chiles
- 1 (14.5-ounce) can fire-roasted tomatoes, undrained
- 1 (10-ounce) can Latin-seasoned tomatoes, undrained
- 1 cup chicken or beef broth
- 3 1/2 pounds beef chuck roast or stew meat cut into 1 1/2 inch cubes
- Salt and pepper to taste

Instructions

1. Place the chiles in a bowl and pour boiling water over them to cover. Let sit for 10 minutes.
2. While the chiles are soaking, heat the oil in a large pot. Add the onion and cook 4–6 minutes or until softened. Add the garlic and cook for 1 minute more, stirring constantly. Add the cumin, oregano, fire-roasted tomatoes, Latin-seasoned tomatoes, and chicken/beef broth to the pot. Turn up the heat to a simmer and cook for 10 minutes.
3. Take the chiles out of the hot water and cut in half; remove the seeds and stems.
4. Place the chiles in a blender along with the tomato mixture and blend until completely smooth. Season to taste with salt and pepper.
5. Season the meat with salt and pepper and place in the slow cooker.
6. Pour your blended sauce all over the meat.
7. Cook on low for 6–8 hours.
8. As he chows down relentlessly, know that you seriously own this dude.

Serve this with warmed corn or flour tortillas, corn chips, chopped white onion, guacamole, chopped cilantro, Mexican cheese blend, sour cream or subtle indifference.

SLOW COOKER TURKEY CHILI

This recipe contains beans. You've been warned.

Total Time 8:15 • Servings: As many as you damn want

Ingredients

- 1 tablespoon olive oil
- 2 pounds lean ground turkey
- 1 medium red or yellow onion, peeled and diced
- 4 cloves garlic, minced
- 2 (15-ounce) cans tomato sauce
- 2 (14-ounce) cans diced tomatoes
- 3 (15-ounce) cans dark red kidney beans, rinsed and drained
- 1 (4-ounce) can chopped green chiles
- 1 cup beef or chicken broth
- 1 packet (1/4 cup) taco seasoning
- 1 tablespoon chili powder
- 1 teaspoon ground cumin
- 1 teaspoon salt
- 1 teaspoon sugar
- 1/2 teaspoon black pepper

Instructions

1. Heat oil in a large sauté pan over medium-high heat. Add the ground turkey and sauté until completely browned, about 6–8 minutes, using a wooden spoon to stir and break up the meat as it cooks. Drain excess liquid, or not, then transfer the turkey to your slow cooker.
2. Add all of the remaining ingredients and stir to combine. Cook on low for 6–8 hours until it's all cooked through.
3. As he's eating and gazing lovingly into your eyes, just think to yourself, "Wow, I barely did a fucking thing to make this."

Note: You can serve this with warmed corn or flour tortillas, over corn chips, or with shredded Mexican cheese blend, chopped white onions, chopped scallions, chopped cilantro, sour cream, salsa, diced avocado, and/or guacamole.

Actually…serve everything with guacamole.

SLOW COOKER SHREDDED CHICKEN TERIYAKI

This dish has all of the sweet and tangy taste of chicken teriyaki with all of the awesomeness of braised, shredded meat. Basically, everything in life that's great.

Total Time 4:10 • Servings: Up to you, I'm no food cop

Ingredients

- 1/2 cup teriyaki sauce
- 1/2 cup chicken broth
- 1/3 cup brown sugar, packed
- 1/4 cup soy sauce
- 4 cloves garlic, minced
- 1 teaspoon sesame oil
- 3 boneless, skinless chicken breasts or thighs, depending on your preference…or, I *suppose,* his.

Instructions

1. In a large bowl, mix together teriyaki sauce, chicken broth, brown sugar, soy sauce, garlic, and sesame oil.
2. Place chicken into slow cooker. Add sauce mixture and toss to combine.
3. Cover and cook on low heat for 3 hours and 30 minutes.
4. Check to make sure chicken is cooked through. Remove chicken from the slow cooker and using two forks, shred the chicken before returning it to the pot with the juices.
5. Cover and keep warm for an additional 30 minutes.
6. Serve immediately.
7. The next time he asks for this, sigh at first, as if it's a lot of trouble.

Serve with thinly sliced green onions and sesame seeds over rice, on buns, or straight out of the slow cooker using a serving fork. You do you!

YOU BARELY HAVE TO CARE
BARBEQUE PULLED PORK
SANDWICHES

As he's devouring this, smile because he'll never know how little you worked on it.

Total Time 6:05 • Servings: Maybe 1, maybe 12

Ingredients

- 1 pork tenderloin, trimmed (about 1 pound)
- 1 jar of his favorite BBQ sauce
- Everyone's favorite Hawaiian rolls
- Store-bought coleslaw

Instructions

1. Pour the sauce in the bottom of the slow cooker.
2. Place the tenderloin in, and spoon sauce over the top.
3. Cook on low for 5–6 hours.
4. Remove meat and shred with two forks.
5. Add the meat back into the slow cooker and combine with the sauce.
6. Place a pile of meat on a Hawaiian roll. Preheat the roll if you're feeling nice.
7. Add a spoonful of coleslaw.
8. Watch your guy devour the shit out of this.

SIMPLY SHREDDED FRENCH DIP

In Los Angeles there are two restaurants that claim to have invented the French Dip Sandwich. One of the restaurants is terrible, the other one is Philippe's. No one truly knows who invented the French Dip Sandwich, but you're about to invent a very happy guy.

Total Time 6:05 • Servings: This is entirely subjective

Ingredients

- 1 boneless beef chuck roast (3 pounds), trimmed
- 1 (10 1/2 ounce) can condensed French onion soup, undiluted
- 1 (10 1/2 ounce) can condensed beef consommé, undiluted
- 1 (10 1/2 ounce) can condensed beef broth, undiluted
- 1 teaspoon beef bouillon granules
- 8–10 French or Italian rolls, split

Instructions

1. Cut the roast in half and place in a 3-quart slow cooker.
2. Combine the soup, consommé, broth, and bouillon; pour over roast.
3. Cover and cook on low for 6–8 hours or until meat is tender.
4. Remove meat and shred with two forks.
5. Serve on rolls.
6. In shallow bowls, place the juice from the slow cooker on the side for dipping.
7. Later that night, tell him you spent hours on your feet cooking for him so he needs to give you a really long foot massage. Be sure to have pre-placed a bottle of peppermint foot massage lotion on your nightstand.

SUPER SEXY SLOW SALSA CHICKEN

Sometimes in the morning, I'm already thinking about dinner. Don't judge me. A super easy way to have a great meal ready for dinner with almost zero effort is to throw a few boneless, skinless chicken breasts or thighs and some of your favorite salsa in the slow cooker early in the day. When it's time for dinner, your house will smell amazing. This is seriously idiot-proof. Trust me, I'm a serious idiot.

Total Time 4:01 • Servings: That is a social construct and does not really exist

Ingredients

- 4 boneless, skinless chicken breasts or thighs (about 2 pounds total)
- 2 cups of your favorite salsa, or his, I guess

Instructions

1. Place chicken in a slow cooker and cover with salsa. Toss until the chicken is covered.
2. Cover and cook on high for 4 hours (or low for 6–8 hours), or until the chicken shreds easily with a fork. Shred the chicken in the slow cooker and toss with the remaining salsa and juices until well mixed.
3. Serve immediately with chips or on tortillas and garnish with shredded cheese, diced tomatoes, cilantro, sour cream . . . whatever the hell you want. After all, you slaved for **minutes** to make this meal.

FUN FOOD FACTS 4

Three of the most popular pastas are:
Penne, Spaghetti and Macaroni.

The least popular: Erwin.

PASTA

Nothing is quite as comforting, satisfying, and nurturing as a heaping plate of fresh, homemade pasta. Unfortunately, I am allergic to gluten, so genuine pasta is never on my menu.

Hey, it's not as if I'd ever want a warm bowl of perfectly al dente, artisanal semolina pasta coated in a bright San Marzano tomato sauce rich with notes of deep roasted fresh garlic, generously dusted with creamy Parmigiano Reggiano cheese and garnished with delicate, hand-torn fresh basil.

Buon appetito, you lucky motherfuckers.

CHEESY CHILI MAC

Mexican seasoning, macaroni, cheese, and meat. Really the holy quaternity of foods. Is quaternity a word? It is now. This is a delicious meal that heats up well the next day. Or later that night after you've boned and you're starving again.

Total Time :30 • Servings: Yes, and they are quite delicious

Ingredients

- 1 pound lean ground beef or turkey
- 1/2 an onion, finely chopped
- 3 cloves garlic, minced
- 1 tablespoon chili powder
- 1 tablespoon ground cumin
- 1 tablespoon brown sugar
- Salt and pepper, to taste
- 2 cups water
- 1 (15-ounce) can tomato sauce
- 8 ounces elbow macaroni (about 2 cups)
- 1 1/2–2 cups Mexican cheese blend, pepper jack, or cheddar
- Chopped cilantro, and diced avocado for garnish

Instructions

1. Heat large skillet over medium heat; add the ground beef/turkey and cook until browned.
2. Just before the meat is cooked through, add the chopped onion.
3. Add the minced garlic and cook for an additional 30 seconds.
4. Add the chili powder, cumin, and brown sugar. Season with salt and pepper.
5. Add the water and tomato sauce; stir well to combine.
6. Stir in the uncooked macaroni, cover pan, and cook until noodles are done, stirring occasionally to prevent sticking to the bottom of the pan.
7. Turn off heat and add the cheese; stir to melt.
8. Garnish with chopped cilantro and diced avocado.
9. Watch him destroy this dinner, and smile knowing how easy it is to destroy a guy.

ONE-POT PASTA MIRACLE

I love one-pot anything because I hate doing dishes. This is a great way to infuse flavor into your pasta while being a totally lazy queen. And you know what, you deserve to work less. You've almost certainly been paid less.

Total Time :20 • Servings: Until it's gone, obvi

Ingredients

- 1 pound spaghetti
- 1 (12.8-ounce) package smoked andouille sausage, thinly sliced on a bias, fancy-style
- 1 large onion, thinly sliced
- 4 1/2 cups water
- 3 cups grape tomatoes, halved
- 2 cups fresh basil leaves, loosely packed
- 4 cloves garlic, thinly sliced like in the movie *Goodfellas*
- Kosher salt and freshly ground black pepper, to taste
- 1 cup Parmesan cheese, grated

Instructions

1. In a large stockpot or Dutch oven over medium-high heat, combine spaghetti, sausage, onion, tomatoes, basil, garlic, and 4 1/2 cups water; season with salt and pepper to taste.
2. Bring to a boil; reduce heat and simmer, uncovered, until pasta is cooked through and liquid has reduced, about 8–10 minutes.
3. Stir in Parmesan.
4. Serve immediately.
5. Pairs nicely with garlic bread, a small green salad, or sanctimonious entitlement.

ONE-POT HALF-HOUR CREAMY TOMATO BASIL PASTA BAKE

Really, with a title that long do I have to elaborate? This shit is great.

Total Time :30 • Servings: Hey, why don't YOU decide?

Ingredients

- 1 pound dry fettuccine or another long-cut pasta
- 1 tablespoon salted butter
- 1 cup store-bought basil pesto
- 1 (28-ounce) jar marinara sauce
- 1/3 cup red enchilada sauce
- 1/2 cup oil-packed sun-dried tomatoes, drained and chopped
- 4 ounces goat cheese, crumbled
- 1 cup fontina cheese, cubed
- 1/2 cup heavy cream
- Kosher salt and pepper
- 6 ounces fresh mozzarella cheese, torn
- 2 cups fresh cherry tomatoes, halved
- 1/2 cup fresh basil leaves

Instructions

1. Preheat oven to 375°F.
2. Bring a large, oven-safe pot of salted water to a boil. Cook the pasta according to package directions until al dente. Drain the pasta and add it right back to the hot pot.
3. To the pot add the butter, pesto, pasta sauce, enchilada sauce, sun-dried tomatoes, goat cheese, fontina cheese, and milk/cream. Season with salt and pepper.
4. Gently toss everything together until a creamy sauce has formed, about 3–5 minutes. Scatter the mozzarella over the pasta.
5. Transfer to the oven and bake for 10–15 minutes, then turn the broiler on and broil for 1–2 minutes or until cheese is golden and bubbly.
6. Remove from oven and let sit 5 minutes. Serve topped with tomatoes and fresh basil.
7. Pairs nicely with gently steamed broccoli tossed with garlic.
8. Pretend to be totally exhausted and make him clean the kitchen.

SUPER SEXY CREAMY MAC AND CHEESE

As simple as it is, that boxed mac with powdered cheese is not good enough for your man. Most of the time. This homemade version is super rich, creamy, and super sexy.

Total Time :30 • Servings: I have no idea how hungry you are, dude

Ingredients

- 1 pound elbow macaroni
- 8 tablespoons butter (1 stick), cut into 1-tablespoon-sized pieces
- 2 cups half-and-half
- 2 cups sharp cheddar cheese, shredded
- 2 cups Monterey Jack cheese, shredded
- 2 eggs, lightly beaten
- 8 ounces shelf-stable meltable boxed cheese, cut into small cubes
- 1/4 teaspoon seasoned salt
- 1/4 teaspoon black pepper

Instructions

1. Preheat oven to 350°F and butter a 9x13-inch casserole dish.
2. Cook pasta until just tender. It will cook more as it bakes.
3. Drain pasta and return to pot. While pasta is still hot, add butter, and stir until butter is melted.
4. Add the half-and-half to the pot, along with half the cheddar and Monterey Jack, the eggs, boxed cheese, seasoned salt, and pepper. Stir to mix well.
5. Pour into prepared dish and sprinkle with remaining cheese.
6. Bake for 30–35 minutes.
7. Serve as a main dish, side dish, dessert, and/or late-night stoner food.

SIMPLE HOMEMADE LASAGNA

Homemade melty warm lasagna can bring a man to his knees. The good news is, once he's down there he can fix the garbage disposal.

Total Time 1:30 • Servings: Yesss!

Ingredients

- 12 fresh lasagna noodles
- 4 cups mozzarella cheese, shredded
- 1/2 cup parmesan cheese, shredded
- 1/2 pound lean ground beef or turkey
- 1/2 pound Italian sausage (pork or turkey)
- 1 onion, diced
- 2 garlic cloves, minced
- 24 ounces pasta sauce
- 2 tablespoons tomato paste
- 1 teaspoon Italian seasoning
- 2 cups ricotta cheese
- 1/4 cup fresh parsley, chopped
- 1 egg, beaten beyond recognition

Instructions

1. Heat oven to 350°F.
2. Brown beef/turkey, sausage, onion, and garlic over medium-high heat until no pink remains. Drain any fat.
3. Stir in pasta sauce, tomato paste, and Italian seasoning. Simmer 5 minutes.
4. In a separate bowl, combine 3 cups mozzarella, ricotta, 1/4 cup parmesan cheese, parsley, and egg.
5. Add 1 cup meat sauce to a 9x13-inch pan. Top with 3 lasagna noodles. Layer with 1/3 of the cheese mixture and 1 cup of meat sauce. Repeat, finishing with noodles topped with sauce.
6. Cover with foil and bake 45 minutes. Uncover, sprinkle on more mozzarella cheese, and bake an additional 15 minutes or until browned and bubbly. Broil 2–3 minutes if desired.
7. Rest 10–15 minutes before cutting.
8. For extra credit, dress like Sophia Loren. Dudes love that.

LINGUINI WITH SHRIMP AND SPINACH

I love recipes that use as few dishes as possible. This one could not be easier because it's all created in one pot. If you're gluten-free like me, you can use a GF pasta. Some of them don't suck.

Total Time :17 • Servings: At least one and maybe four

Ingredients

- 3/4 pound linguini
- 1 pound medium shrimp, peeled and deveined
- 1 tablespoon extra-virgin olive oil, plus more for drizzling
- 1 tablespoon lemon zest
- 2 tablespoons lemon juice
- 4 cups baby spinach
- Coarse salt and ground pepper

Instructions

1. In a large pot of boiling salted water, cook the linguini according to package instructions.
2. In the last 3 minutes of cooking, add shrimp to the pot and cook until opaque throughout.
3. Drain the pasta and shrimp and then return to the pot.
4. Toss with olive oil, lemon zest, lemon juice, and spinach.
5. Season with salt and pepper and drizzle with oil.
6. Eat as much as you want because the BMI is a totally fake social construct created by the diet industry to make you feel bad about your awesome body so you'll buy all of their diet shit. You look awesome, girl!

CAVATELLI AND BROCCOLI

This dish sounds like a 1980s TV drama starring Dennis Farina as a grizzled police detective begrudgingly assigned a rookie partner who's a stalk of fresh broccoli. Together they solve crimes and are an excellent source of fiber. Fridays at 10!

Total Time :40 • Servings: I mean, it's really good so who knows?

Ingredients

- 2 pounds bite-size broccoli florets
- 1/4 cup extra-virgin olive oil, divided
- 1 teaspoon kosher salt, plus additional to taste
- 1/4 teaspoon black pepper, plus additional to taste
- 1 (15-ounce) can cannellini beans or other white beans
- 8 ounces cavatelli
- 1 medium lemon, zested and juiced
- 1/2 teaspoon freshly ground black pepper
- 1 cup ricotta cheese (about 7 1/2 ounces)
- 1/4 cup Parmesan cheese, grated, plus additional for serving
- 1/4 teaspoon red pepper flakes, plus additional to taste

Instructions

1. Place a rack in the center of your oven and preheat to 400°F.
2. Place the broccoli and white beans on a cookie sheet in the center.
3. Drizzle with olive oil and sprinkle with salt and black pepper. Toss to coat, then spread in an even layer, scattering the beans throughout. Roast for 15 minutes, then remove the pan from the oven and gently toss the broccoli and beans to promote even browning.
4. Return to the oven and bake 5–10 additional minutes, until the broccoli is dark and crisp at the tips of the florets and the beans are lightly crisp. Set aside.
5. While the broccoli and beans cook, bring a large pot of salted water to a boil.
6. Add the pasta and cook until al dente, according to the package instructions. Reserve 1 cup of the pasta cooking water, then drain the pasta.
7. Return the pasta to the pot. Add 1/4 cup reserved pasta cooking water, the ricotta, parmesan, red pepper flakes, and remaining 1/4 teaspoon salt.
8. Zest the lemon right into the pot, then cut the lemon into quarters and squeeze in the juice. Add the roasted broccoli and beans, then gently stir, adding more pasta water as needed if the sauce is too thick. Taste and add more seasoning as desired.
9. Serve hot, sprinkled with additional parmesan cheese.
10. If he asks you if you're trying to fatten him up, just laugh and smile. That will confuse him, which is generally pretty easy to do.

MEAT

No offense to vegans, vegetarians, pescatarians, or undeclared, but meat is quite delicious. Here are several recipes that will tame and impress the carnivore in your bed.

SALT AND PEPPER SKIRT STEAK

Not to be confused with Salt-N-Pepa skirt steak, but you'll still want to get up on this super easy way to make a steak dinner even my mother couldn't ruin. Maybe.

Total Time :17 • Servings: Mmmmm, meat

Ingredients

- 1 pound skirt steak
- Salt and pepper

Instructions

1. Season the skirt steak with salt and pepper.
2. In a cast-iron skillet over medium to medium-high heat, place the skirt steak. Slightly press down to create sear. For medium rare, cook for 3 minutes. Flip steak and cook for an additional 3 minutes. If you prefer your steak more well done, cook for longer. Duh!
3. Let steak rest about 10 minutes, then cut thin slices against the grain.
4. You are now a steak cooking mo-fo!

PERFECT PORK CHOPS

Properly cooked, pork chops can be juicy and delicious. Be sure to take your pork chops out of the refrigerator about 15 minutes before you plan to start cooking. Bringing the meat up to room temperature first is the key to even cooking. See? You actually learned something here!

Total Time :30 • Servings: Can you eat 4 pork chops by yourself? If you can, that's awesome

Ingredients

- 1 teaspoon paprika
- 1/2 teaspoon thyme leaves
- 1/2 teaspoon salt
- 1/4 teaspoon ground black pepper
- 4 pork chops (bone-in or boneless)
- 1 teaspoon extra virgin olive oil

Instructions

1. Mix paprika, thyme, salt, and black pepper in a small bowl. Sprinkle evenly over both sides of pork chops.
2. Heat a large cast-iron frying pan to medium-high or high heat (hot enough to sear the meat).
3. If using bone-in chops, score the fat that surrounds the chops with a couple vertical cuts to help prevent the chops from buckling as they cook.
4. Once the pan is hot, add a teaspoon of oil or fat to the pan and coat the bottom of the pan. Right before you put the pork chops into the pan, sprinkle each side with a little salt, or you can salt the chops in the pan.
5. Place the pork chops with the thickest, boniest parts toward the center of the pan where they get the most heat. Make sure the chops are not crowding each other too much.
6. You may need to cook them in batches. There should be space between the chops in the pan, or the meat will steam and not sear properly.
7. Sear the pork chops, about 2 minutes on each side. Watch carefully—as soon as the chops are browned, flip them. As soon as you flip the pork chops, if you are using a cast-iron pan, you can turn off the heat. Cast iron holds heat very well, and there will be enough heat in the pan to finish cooking the meat.
8. If you have chops that are a lot thicker than 3/4 inch (many are sold that are 1 1/2 inches thick), you can put a cover on the pan and let the pork chops finish cooking for 5 minutes or so.
9. Check the internal temperature of the pork with a digital thermometer; when the pork registers 145°F in the middle, it's done.
10. Mmmmmmm, pork!

MELTY MOZZARELLA STUFFED
BARBEQUE MEATLOAF

I have always loved meatloaf that was not prepared by my mother. This one is next-level, thanks to a gooey, melty layer of cheese in the middle. Use your guy's favorite barbeque sauce for the glaze and he just might faint from food bliss.

Total Time 1:10 • Servings: Until it's gone

Ingredients

- 1 pound lean ground beef or ground turkey
- 1 cup dried breadcrumbs
- 1/2 cup yellow onion, diced
- 1/2 cup milk
- 1 large egg, beaten
- 4 tablespoons of your favorite salsa
- 3/4 teaspoon salt
- 1/2 teaspoon garlic powder
- 1/4 teaspoon ground black pepper
- 8 ounces fresh mozzarella, sliced
- 1 cup of your guy's favorite barbeque sauce

Instructions

1. Preheat oven to 350°F. Place parchment paper over a baking sheet.
2. In a large bowl, add the ground beef/turkey, breadcrumbs, onion, milk, egg, salsa, salt, garlic powder, and pepper. Use your hands to mix these ingredients together until well combined.
3. Divide meat in half. Shape one half of the meat into the bottom half of the meatloaf on the baking sheet. Place mozzarella slices down the center, leaving 1/2 inch around the ends and sides. Shape remaining half of meat as the top half of the loaf, sealing the edges. You don't have to be perfect, this is going to turn out great.
4. Pour half of the barbeque sauce over the top of the meatloaf, reserving the remaining half for later.
5. Bake for 45 minutes.
6. After 45 minutes, remove from oven and pour the remaining sauce over the loaf. Increase temperature to 400°F and bake for an additional 15 minutes.
7. Let rest 5–10 minutes before serving.
8. Pairs nicely with peas, mashed potatoes, and a chocolate brownie.
9. Serve on metal TV dinner trays for extra realness.

PERFECT PAN-SEARED STEAK

Nothing says "I love you" to a guy quite like a perfectly cooked hunk of meat on a plate. Learn how to make the perfect stovetop steak, and you'll always have someone joining you for dinner.

Total Time :25 • Servings: All of them are great

Ingredients

- 1 boneless ribeye steak or sirloin, at least 1 1/2 pounds, cut to at least 1 1/2 inches thick
- Pinch of salt
- Freshly ground black pepper
- 2 teaspoons extra-virgin olive oil
- 3 tablespoons butter
- 2 garlic cloves, peeled and left whole
- A few sprigs of fresh parsley, including stems

Instructions

1. Salt and pepper one side of the steak.
2. Heat your cast-iron skillet until smoking hot. Add oil and swirl around to coat. Add steak seasoned side down (place it in the pan away from you so you don't get splattered), and then salt and pepper the other side of the steak. Do not touch it for two minutes.
3. Using tongs (never pierce the meat with a fork), flip the steak and add butter, garlic, and parsley to the pan next to the steak. Allow the steak to cook for 2 more minutes.
4. Right after you flip the steak for the first time, with a spoon or small ladle, keep basting the melted butter over the steak. Baste continually for the full two minutes (tilt pan a little if you have to, to get the butter onto the spoon).
5. After two minutes on each side, keep flipping and basting the steak each time, leaving the steak for 30 seconds before turning. Test the steak with the poke test (see below) and remove at medium-rare, about the 5–6 minutes total cooking time. Cook a minute or two longer for medium to well. A thicker steak (such as a sirloin) may take longer.
6. Turn off the heat and baste one more time. Leave the steak in the pan loosely covered with foil for 10 minutes and allow to rest before cutting. Baste one more time and remove to a cutting board. For a nice presentation, slice on the bias and serve slices.
7. This dinner is currency, spend it wisely.

Poke Test: Make a relaxed fist. The fleshy area of your hand between your thumb and forefinger is soft, which is how a rare steak feels. If you slightly clench your fist, it's a little firmer, like medium doneness. Clench your fist tightly, and the area will feel like well-done.

THE EASIEST, FASTEST SWEDISH
MEATBALLS EVER

Like everything else Swedish, this is a meal you have to assemble yourself. However, I made it easy with premade meatballs and no hex wrenches. Extra points if you're seated in Poäng chairs while dining.

Total :20 • Servings: Depends on how many balls you like in your mouth

Ingredients

- 1 cup beef stock
- 1 cup heavy cream
- 3 tablespoons all-purpose flour
- 1 tablespoon soy sauce
- 1 teaspoon ground black pepper
- 1/2 teaspoon dried rosemary
- 1/2 (20-ounce) package frozen cooked meatballs, thawed

Instructions

1. Whisk together the beef stock, heavy cream, flour, soy sauce, black pepper, and rosemary in a large saucepan until smooth.
2. Cook and stir over low heat until thickened, about 10 minutes, stirring occasionally.
3. Stir in the premade meatballs and continue cooking until meatballs are heated through and nicely coated, about 5 more minutes.
4. Pairs nicely with boiled potatoes, lingonberry jam, or honungsglaserade rödbetor.

STEAK KABOBS

Everything tastes better when it's served on a stick. Except cereal. These kabobs are easy to make, visually striking, and as much fun to say as they are to eat. Plus, you get a greasy weapon when you're done!

Total Time :35 • Servings: You kabob you, bro

Ingredients

- 2 ribeye steaks (1 1/2 to 2 pounds total), trimmed of excess fat and cut into chunks
- 2 tablespoons olive oil
- 1 tablespoon lime juice
- Sea salt (about 1 teaspoon, or to taste)
- Pinch black pepper
- 1/2 teaspoon ground cumin
- 1/2 teaspoon paprika
- 2 cloves garlic, pressed through garlic press
- 1/2 small red onion, cut into small chunks
- 1 cup cherry tomatoes
- Skewers—if made of wood, make sure they're presoaked in water

Instructions

1. Add the trimmed, cubed steak into a bowl, along with the olive oil, lime juice, salt, pepper, cumin, paprika, and garlic, and toss well to coat.
2. Assemble the skewers by adding a piece of the red onion, followed by some steak, then tomato, then more onion, steak, tomato to each skewer until all ingredients are used. You should have about 6 skewers.
3. Allow the skewers to marinate for at least an hour, or better yet, overnight.
4. Once you're ready to cook, place a grill pan over medium-high heat. Drizzle in a little oil and grill the kabobs for about 6–8 minutes, turning them to char on each side, or until medium rare.
5. Serve hot with delicious sides such as saffron rice, middle eastern salad, or pita bread.
6. As he eats, casually mention that kabob is believed to have originated in Turkey, where soldiers would grill chunks of meat on their swords over open fires. This will make him feel manlier . . . and hopefully less bloated.

GRANDMA'S BEEF STEW

My grandmother could take five disparate items in the refrigerator and turn them into a feast. I don't have her skills, but at least I know how to use a DVD player.

Total Time 3:20 • Servings: Thanks, I will have some

Ingredients

- 1/4 cup all-purpose flour
- 1/4 teaspoon freshly ground pepper
- 1 pound beef stewing meat, trimmed and cut into 1-inch cubes
- 5 teaspoons vegetable oil
- 2 tablespoons red wine vinegar
- 1 cup red wine
- 3 1/2 cups low-sodium canned beef broth
- 2 bay leaves
- 1 medium onion, peeled and chopped
- 5 medium carrots, peeled and cut into 1/2-inch rounds
- 2 large Yukon gold potatoes, peeled and cut into 3/4-inch cubes
- 2 teaspoons salt

Instructions

1. Combine the flour and pepper in a bowl, add the beef cubes, and toss to coat well. Heat 3 teaspoons of the oil in a Dutch oven that has a cover. Add the beef a few pieces at a time; do not overcrowd. Cook, turning the pieces until beef is seared on all sides. Add more oil as needed between batches.
2. Remove the beef from the pot and add the vinegar and wine. Cook over medium-high heat, scraping the pan with a wooden spoon to incorporate any of the browned bits. Add the seared beef, beef broth, and bay leaves. Bring to a boil, then reduce to a low and slow simmer.
3. Cover and cook until the beef is tender, about 1 1/2 hours. Add the onions and carrots and simmer, covered, for 10 more minutes. Add the potatoes and simmer until vegetables are tender, about 30 minutes more. If the stew begins to dry out, add more beef broth or water. Season with salt and pepper to taste.
4. Serve in his favorite bowl and watch him try not to faint from happiness.

FUN FOOD FACTS 5

Chicken pot pie is the perfect dinner.

If you add commas.

POULTRY

The O.G. White Meat.

LEMON GRILLED CHICKEN BREASTS

This dish might not sound all that aspirational but it's actually the perfect boneless dinner for a night of boning. Lemon makes everything taste fresh. I'm a big fan of the Pledge.

Total Time :38 • Servings: Just how hungry are you?

Ingredients

- 3 tablespoons fresh lemon juice
- 2 tablespoons olive oil
- 2 garlic cloves, minced
- 4 boneless, skinless chicken breasts or thighs
- Salt and pepper

Instructions

1. Place the lemon juice, olive oil, and garlic in a plastic zipper bag and add the chicken. Seal and flip the bag around a few times to make sure all of the chicken is coated in some of the marinade. Place the bag in the refrigerator for 30 minutes.
2. Preheat your grill pan on high heat. Remove the chicken

from the marinade and salt and pepper both sides. Grill for 4 minutes on one side and then flip and grill for another 3–4 minutes or until chicken is cooked through.

Safety Note: The USDA recommends that chicken and poultry be cooked to a minimum internal temperature of 165°F for at least 30 seconds, but white meat and dark meat are typically done at different temperatures. Some chefs suggest white meat is properly cooked when it reaches 150°F for at least three minutes, and 175°F for dark meat. Please don't kill anyone with undercooked chicken.

GRILLED CHICKEN AND ZUCCHINI KABOBS

These light chicken kabobs have tons of flavor and not as much fat as red meat. Remember, if you're using wooden skewers, soak them in water first. If you're using metal skewers, you were smart when you bought them that one time. See?

Total Time :40 • Servings: I have no idea how hungry you are right now, sorry

Ingredients

- 2 boneless chicken breasts or thighs, cut into 1-inch pieces
- 2 medium zucchinis, sliced into thick rounds
- 1 large red onion, cut into 1-inch pieces
- 2 large lemons
- 3 cloves garlic, minced
- 1 tablespoon chopped fresh thyme
- 1 tablespoon chopped fresh rosemary
- 1 tablespoon olive oil
- 1 teaspoon kosher salt
- 1/2 teaspoon freshly ground pepper

Instructions

1. Place the chicken pieces in a plastic zipper bag. Place the zucchini and red onion in a separate plastic zipper bag or bowl. Set aside.
2. Zest one of the lemons and place the zest in a medium bowl. Juice both lemons and add to the lemon zest. Add the minced garlic, thyme, rosemary, olive oil, salt, and pepper. Whisk the marinade together. Pour half of the marinade into the bag with the chicken pieces and pour the other half in the bag with the zucchini and onion. Let marinate for 30 minutes or up to 4 hours in the refrigerator.
3. When ready to prepare, skewer the kabobs. Alternate chicken, zucchini, and onion on the skewers. Discard any remaining marinade.
4. Lightly brush your grill pan with olive oil and preheat to medium heat.
5. Grill chicken kabobs, turning often so each side browns and has light grill marks, about 10–12 minutes or until chicken is cooked through. Serve immediately.
6. Make sure chicken has reached the proper internal temperature before eating.
7. Serve in pita or with a Mediterranean salad or rice. Or all of it!
8. Nostimo!

SHEET PAN CHICKEN WITH SWEET POTATOES AND BRUSSELS SPROUTS

This rustic and satisfying meal hits every note, and by using only one sheet pan, cleanup is a breeze. It's an even bigger breeze if you make him do the cleanup.

Total Time :55 • Servings: That's on you, girl

Ingredients

- 4 boneless, skinless chicken breasts, lightly pounded with the flat side of a meat mallet or rolling pin to an even 1/4-inch thickness
- 3 tablespoons extra-virgin olive oil
- 4 cloves garlic, minced
- 2 tablespoons fresh rosemary, chopped
- 1 teaspoon kosher salt
- 1/2 teaspoon black pepper
- 1 pound brussels sprouts, trimmed and halved
- 1 large sweet potato, peeled and cut into 1/2-inch cubes
- 1 medium red onion, cut into 1/2-inch pieces

Instructions

1. Preheat oven to 425°F.
2. Place the pounded chicken breasts in a large plastic zipper bag. Drizzle with 1 1/2 tablespoons olive oil, then add the garlic, 1 tablespoon rosemary, 1/2 teaspoon salt, and 1/4 teaspoon black pepper. Zip the bag tightly, then shake and rub the bag to coat the chicken in the oil and spices. Set aside while you chop the vegetables.
3. Once chopped, place the brussels sprouts, sweet potato, and onion on a large rimmed baking sheet. Drizzle with the remaining 1 1/2 tablespoons olive oil, then sprinkle with remaining 1/2 teaspoon kosher salt and 1/4 teaspoon black pepper. Toss to evenly coat, then spread in an even layer.
4. Remove the chicken from the marinade and place on top of the vegetables. Place in the oven and roast until the chicken is cooked through and the internal temperature reaches 160 to 165°F, about 18–22 minutes. Once the chicken is cooked through, remove to a plate to rest. Cover with foil to keep warm. Return the pan of vegetables to the oven to continue baking until caramelized and tender, about 10–15 additional minutes. Sprinkle with the remaining 1 tablespoon fresh rosemary. Serve warm with the rested chicken.
5. It's meals like this that will keep your guy happy—as long as he likes chicken and brussels sprouts, that is.

EASY BREEZY CHICKEN TACOS

Tacos are the single greatest invention in the history of the world. Lightbulbs and wheels are cool but they're just not tacos.

Total Time 2:15 • Servings: For me, maybe all

Ingredients

- 2 large boneless, skinless chicken breasts
- 1 clove garlic, minced
- 1 1/2 tablespoons chili powder
- 1 tablespoon cumin
- 2 tablespoons plus 1/4 cup hot sauce
- 1 lime (juice and zest)
- 1 tablespoon olive oil
- Salt and pepper
- Soft or hardshell corn tortillas
- Cilantro, chopped
- Avocado, diced, or premade guacamole
- Small white onion, diced
- Iceberg lettuce, shredded
- Mexican blend cheese, shredded

Instructions

1. In a plastic zipper bag, combine garlic, chili powder, cumin, lime juice, lime zest, a squirt of hot sauce, olive oil, salt, and pepper.
2. Add chicken and let marinate for at least 2 hours in refrigerator.
3. Heat a heavy-duty grill pan to high heat for about 2–3 minutes. Lower the heat to medium-high and add the oil to the pan, making sure the entire pan is coated with oil.
4. Add the chicken breasts to the pan and cook for 5–6 minutes on the first side without moving, until the undersides develop dark grill marks. Flip the chicken breasts using a pair of tongs and cook the other side for 5–6 minutes. Make sure they're fully cooked.
5. Let chicken rest for 10 minutes and then use a fork to shred.
6. Warm up soft tortillas in a skillet and prepare all of the toppings in individual bowls.
7. To assemble the tacos, place shredded chicken in a tortilla and top with cheese, lettuce, cilantro, onion, avocado, and hot sauce (or whatever toppings you prefer).
8. After he enjoys this South-of-the-Border treat, he'll spend the next few hours South of Your Border, if you know what I mean.

NO JIVE TURKEY SHEPHERD'S PIE

This is the easiest version of shepherd's pie ever. He'll never know you went prefab. Just to be safe, you might want to mess up a few extra pots and try your best to look exhausted. Trust me, it will pay off later.

Total Time :40 • Servings: Until you cannot move anymore

Ingredients

- 1/2 (13-ounce) box mashed potatoes
- The ingredients required to make them on the box: butter, milk, and salt
- 1 pound ground turkey
- 12-ounce bag frozen mixed veggies
- 1 (10.75-ounce) can tomato soup
- 1 (1.5-ounce) packet beef stew seasoning mix
- 1/2 cup water
- 1 cup cheddar cheese, shredded

Instructions

1. Preheat oven to 400°F.
2. Prepare the mashed potatoes according to the package directions for 10 servings.
3. Brown the ground turkey in a large skillet. Drain any excess grease.
4. Add the can of tomato soup, frozen mixed veggies, beef stew seasoning mix, and water to the browned turkey; stir and simmer for 5–10 minutes on low heat.
5. Spread the ground turkey mixture onto the bottom of a greased 9x13 baking dish.
6. Evenly spread the prepared mashed potatoes over the top, and then sprinkle with cheese.
7. Bake uncovered in the center rack for about 30 minutes, or until the cheese starts to brown.
8. Your dinner is the shepherd, he shall want it again and again.

BEYOND-EASY BAKED TURKEY MEATBALLS

These are a go-to dinner in my house. Once again, you want to give the *illusion* that you worked super hard on this, but really, this is a super-fast and easy recipe. There are tons of ways you can serve these balls, but remember that they can be delicate. Always be gentle with the balls.

Total Time :45 • Servings: Mmmmm, balls

Ingredients

- 1 pound lean ground turkey
- 1/2 cup Italian-style breadcrumbs
- 1/2 cup fresh parmesan cheese, grated
- 1 teaspoon onion powder
- 1 teaspoon garlic salt
- 1 teaspoon Italian seasoning
- 1/4 cup milk
- 1 egg, beaten

Instructions

1. Heat oven to 375°F. Spray large cookie sheet with cooking spray.
2. In large bowl, mix turkey, breadcrumbs, cheese, onion powder, garlic salt, and Italian seasoning. Add milk and egg; mix until just combined. Do not overmix, or they won't be tender.
3. Shape mixture into 15 balls of slightly less than 1/4 cup each. Place on cookie sheet.
4. Bake 16–20 minutes or until thermometer inserted in center of meatballs reads at least 165°F. Serve with pasta and marinara sauce, alongside steamed veggies, or on a hoagie roll with provolone cheese.
5. Any way you can get 'em, you'll want these balls in your mouth.

HOT AND SEXY FRIED CHICKEN TENDERS

Many people believe that spicy food is an aphrodisiac. It warms you up, gets your heart pumping, and increases blood flow. These spicy fried chicken tenders might be the perfect start to a very sweaty night.

Total Time 2:30 • Servings: Good luck not chowing down on all of these in one sitting

Ingredients

- 3 pounds boneless chicken tenders
- 1 cup Frank's RedHot Original Cayenne Pepper Sauce
- 1 1/2 cups all-purpose flour
- 1 1/2 tablespoons Cajun seasoning
- Canola or peanut oil for deep-frying

Instructions

1. Place the chicken tenders in a plastic zipper bag. Pour the hot sauce in the bag and coat the chicken thoroughly.
2. Seal the bag and let it marinate in the refrigerator for 2 hours. Jiggle the bag occasionally to make sure all of the pieces are well coated.
3. In a shallow baking dish, add the AP flour and Cajun seasoning. Combine.
4. Heat about 1/2 inch of oil in a deep heavy skillet to about 360°F.
5. Dredge the marinated chicken tenders in the flour mix.
6. Fry several chicken tenders at a time. Don't overcrowd the skillet. Turn several times with tongs, until deep golden brown, about 6–8 minutes for each batch.
7. Spicy chicken will lead to a spicy relationship. (But maybe avoid mouth-based sexy fun time after this one, trust me.)

FUN FOOD FACTS 6

It's a well-known fact that eating 1-2 servings
of seafood every week is very healthy.

It ain't so healthy for the seafood,
but it's good for you.

SEAFOOD

Neptune was the Roman God of Waters and Seas. He created waves, summoned wind, and carried a super manly trident.

Neptune was a badass.

If he enjoyed seafood, your guy should as well.

Also, a properly butterflied lobster tail
looks exactly like an aroused vulva.

Mmmm, dig in, fellas!

SEARED AHI TUNA STEAKS

This is one of my husband's all-time favorite dishes, and it's incredibly easy. Like me. One day we hope to move to Hawaii and eat fresh-caught tuna every day in between surfing competitions and taking hula dancing lessons on the beach with our blended family and closeted lesbian housekeeper. Although, if I ever find a Tiki idol, I will not wear it around my neck.

Total Time :17 • Servings: Thoroughly theoretical

Ingredients

- 2 (5-ounce) ahi tuna steaks
- 1 teaspoon kosher salt
- 1/4 teaspoon cayenne pepper
- 1/2 tablespoon butter
- 2 tablespoons olive oil
- 1 teaspoon whole peppercorns

Instructions

1. Season the tuna steaks with salt and cayenne pepper.
2. Melt the butter with the olive oil in a skillet over medium-high heat. Cook the peppercorns in the mixture until they soften and pop, about 5 minutes.
3. Gently place the seasoned tuna in the skillet and cook to desired doneness, 1 1/2 minutes per side for rare.
4. Serve with sautéed spinach and mushrooms for extra credit.
5. If you ever find a Tiki idol, leave it.

SUPER FAB CRAB CAKES

You don't have to be in Baltimore to get amazing crab cakes. However, you *do* have to be in Baltimore if you want John Waters to appear on your TV show. At least I did.

Total Time 1:00 • Servings: Will all be so damn good

Ingredients

- 1 large egg
- 1/4 cup mayonnaise
- 2 teaspoons dried parsley
- 2 teaspoons Dijon mustard
- 2 teaspoons Worcestershire sauce
- 1 teaspoon Old Bay seasoning
- 1 teaspoon fresh lemon juice, plus more for serving
- 1/8 teaspoon salt
- 1 pound fresh lump crabmeat (if fresh is not available, canned crabmeat that's drained, flaked, with cartilage removed will also work)
- 2/3 cup saltine cracker crumbs (about 14 crackers)
- Optional: 2 tablespoons salted butter, melted

Instructions

1. Whisk the egg, mayonnaise, parsley, Dijon mustard, Worcestershire sauce, Old Bay, lemon juice, and salt together in a large bowl. Place the crabmeat on top, followed by the cracker crumbs. Very gently and carefully fold together. Try not to break up the crabmeat.
2. Cover tightly and refrigerate for at least 30 minutes and up to 1 day.
3. Preheat oven to 450°F. Generously grease a rimmed baking sheet with nonstick spray.
4. Using a 1/2-cup measuring cup, portion the crab cake mixture into 6 mounds on the baking sheet. (Don't flatten!) Use your hands to gently compact each individual mound so there aren't any lumps sticking out. Brush each mound with melted butter.
5. Bake for 12–14 minutes or until lightly browned around the edges and on top.
6. Drizzle each with fresh lemon juice and serve warm. If you want to serve with store-bought aioli, go ahead. You're busy! You just fucking made crab cakes!
7. Leftover crab cakes can be refrigerated for up to 5 days, but there won't be any leftovers, so there's no point in even wondering about this.

SEARED SALMON WITH FRESH DILL SAUCE

Salmon is loaded with heart-healthy omega-3 fatty acids, protein, and selenium. But it can be a bit intimidating to buy. In some instances, it's actually better to purchase frozen salmon fillets than the "fresh" ones in your grocer's case. If it's been vacuum-sealed and flash-frozen immediately after harvest, it may actually taste fresher than the fish sitting in the supermarket. No offense, dead, stinky fish. I'm sure you're living your best life.

Total Time :15 • Servings: It's four fillets, you do the math

Ingredients

- 1 tablespoon canola oil
- 4 (6-ounce) salmon fillets
- 1 teaspoon Italian seasoning
- 1/4 teaspoon salt
- 1/2 cup plain yogurt
- 1/4 cup mayonnaise
- 1/4 cup cucumber, finely chopped
- 1 teaspoon fresh dill

Instructions

1. In a large skillet, heat oil over medium-high heat.
2. Sprinkle salmon with Italian seasoning and salt.
3. Place in skillet, skin side down. Reduce heat to medium. Cook until fish just begins to flake easily with a fork, about 5 minutes on each side.
4. To create the fresh dill sauce, in a small bowl, combine yogurt, mayonnaise, cucumber, and dill.
5. Drizzle the sauce over the salmon.
6. Watch as your guy enjoys this winner of a dinner.

TRAMPY SHRIMP SCAMPI

I'm calling this dish trampy because once he gets his mouth on it, you're next. Also, it's important you enjoy this dish together so your garlic levels are compatible. #CouplesGoals

Total Time :15 • Servings: I'm not the boss of you

Ingredients

- 4 tablespoons butter
- 1 tablespoon olive oil
- 3 cloves garlic, thoroughly minced
- 1/4 teaspoon crushed red pepper flakes
- 1 pound shrimp, peeled and deveined
- 1/2 cup pinot grigio or sauvignon blanc
- 1/2 cup parsley, chopped
- Kosher salt and freshly ground pepper to taste

Instructions

1. Add the butter and olive oil to a large skillet over medium heat.
2. Stir in the garlic. Cook for 1 minute.
3. Add the shrimp to the pan and toss to coat. Cook the shrimp until bright pink and no longer translucent, approximately 2–3 minutes.
4. Using a slotted spoon, transfer the shrimp to a bowl and cover with foil to keep warm.
5. Add the wine to the pan and cook it down for 2–3 minutes. Turn off the heat.
6. Return the shrimp to the pan and toss to coat in the sauce.
7. Sprinkle with the parsley. Season with salt and pepper to taste.
8. Serve immediately.
9. After the food coma, the fun begins!

ONE COOL CATFISH

Catfish can be polarizing, some either love it or hate it. I'm on Team Catfish and really enjoy it, which is interesting because I'm allergic to cats. I usually pan fry my catfish, but baking it makes a lot less mess and still tastes terrific.

Total Time :25 • Servings: Let God be your guide

Ingredients

- 1/4 cup extra-virgin olive oil
- 1 cup cornmeal
- 1 tablespoon Cajun seasoning
- 4 catfish fillets
- Kosher salt and freshly ground pepper to taste
- Lemon wedges
- Store-bought tartar sauce

Instructions

1. Preheat oven to 425°F.
2. Drizzle 2 tablespoons oil on a large baking sheet.
3. In a shallow baking dish, combine cornmeal and Cajun seasoning.
4. Season catfish with salt and pepper, then dredge fish in seasoned cornmeal, pressing to coat.
5. Place fish on prepared baking sheet and drizzle with remaining 2 tablespoons oil.
6. Bake until golden and fish flakes easily with a fork, about 15 minutes.
7. Serve with lemon wedges and store-bought tartar sauce.
8. Know that you are now the Big Cat when it comes to catfish.

FUN FOOD FACTS 7

**I want someone to look at me
the way I look at bacon.**

BREAKFAST

It turns out, breakfast is actually *not* the most important meal of the day. That "fact" was completely made up by breakfast cereal manufacturers.

For some reason, we totally bought it.

Experts do agree that breakfast is definitely the most FUN meal of the day. Here are a few funlicious ways to start your day.

WAFFLE TOTS EPIC BREAKFAST SANDWICH

This is a mashup of all things delicious for breakfast with help from your trusty waffle iron. Every bite is a happy, cheesy, melty, crispy, yummy foodgasm.

Total Time :21 • Servings: Not nearly enough

Ingredients

- 1 bag frozen potato tots, thawed (you will need 20 ounces or more, depending on the size of your waffle iron)
- 4–6 slices bacon, cooked
- 4–6 slices cheddar or American cheese (or 1/2 cup cheddar cheese, shredded)
- 4 eggs

Instructions

1. Generously coat your waffle iron with nonstick spray and preheat on high.
2. Place the thawed potato tots very close together in an even layer on the waffle iron. Close the lid and press it down, using an oven mitt or a kitchen towel to protect your hands.
3. Cook until the potato tot waffle is crisp, about 5–10 minutes. (The exact time will depend on your waffle iron.)
4. Remove the waffle from the iron and allow to cool on a wire rack.
5. Repeat the process to make a second potato tot waffle.
6. As the second waffle is cooking, prepare eggs your guy's favorite way (as long as it's scrambled or fried, 'cause you ain't got time for all that other bullshit).
7. When the second waffle is done, top it with half of the cheese, the cooked bacon, and then the eggs.
8. Top that with the remaining cheese and place the first waffle on top.
9. Using the bottom plate of the waffle iron, heat the sandwich until the cheese melts.
10. Cut it into quarters and serve.
11. Watch him faint from happiness.

CHEESY BAKED EGGS OVER GRITS

When it comes to cooking eggs, I've discovered that my oven is my best friend. Or at least my best friend when it comes to cooking a bunch of eggs all at once. This recipe is highly scalable for big crowds or hungry eaters.

Prep Time :15 • Servings: Yes

Ingredients

- Cooking spray
- 4 large eggs
- 1/2 cup Quick Grits
- 2 cups water
- Salt to taste
- 2 tablespoons salted butter
- 1/3 cup cheddar cheese, shredded
- 2 tablespoons scallions for garnish, sliced

Instructions

1. Preheat oven to 350°F.
2. Generously spray 4 muffin tin cups with cooking spray.
3. Crack one egg in each cup.
4. Cover each egg with shredded cheddar cheese.
5. Place in oven for 14 minutes (if you prefer your eggs softer or harder, adjust time in the oven accordingly).
6. While eggs are cooking, bring 2 cups of water to a boil.
7. Slowly stir grits and salt into boiling water.
8. Reduce heat to medium-low and cover. Cook 5–7 minutes until thickened, stirring occasionally.
9. Add butter to grits.
10. Remove from heat.
11. When the eggs are done, remove from oven and let rest.
12. Portion the hot cooked grits into two deep bowls.
13. Place two baked eggs on each bowl of grits.
14. Garnish with scallions.
15. Enjoy the fact that you are the breakfast-makingest mofo you know.

SPINACH BREAKFAST TACOS

I don't know if I mentioned it, but I really LOVE tacos. And my very favorite tacos are breakfast tacos! I first experienced this delicacy in the epicenter of breakfast taco magic: Austin, Texas. When I got home to LA, I convinced my favorite Mexican restaurant to put them on their menu. I guess if you eat in a place five times a week, they give you special treatment. *¡Qué ricos tacos!*

Total Time :20 • Servings: 4, but for me, 2?

Ingredients

- 6 eggs, beaten
- 2 cups spinach, chopped
- Extra-virgin olive oil, for drizzling
- Sea salt and freshly ground black pepper
- 8 corn tortillas
- 1/2 cup shredded cheddar or Mexican blend cheese
- Fresh guacamole
- Your favorite store-bought salsa
- 1 scallion, chopped

Instructions

1. Wrap your tortillas in foil and warm them in the oven.
2. Brush a large nonstick skillet lightly with olive oil and bring to medium heat. Add the eggs, let them cook for a few seconds, and then stir. Salt and pepper to taste. Continue to stir and scramble the eggs until just set.
3. Remove the pan from the heat while the eggs are slightly runny and stir in the spinach.
4. Remove warmed tortillas from the oven.
5. Assemble the tacos with the eggs, cheese, guacamole, scallions, and your favorite salsa.
6. Call me!

GLUTEN-FREE ALMOND MEAL SPINACH AND MUSHROOM QUICHE

Real men do like quiche. Especially if it's served in a cast-iron skillet that can be weaponized.

Total Time 1:15 • Servings: It's the size that matters

Ingredients

- 2 cups packed almond meal
- 3 garlic cloves, pressed or minced
- 1 teaspoon dried thyme
- 1/2 teaspoon salt
- 1/4 teaspoon freshly ground pepper
- 1/3 cup olive oil
- 1 tablespoon plus 1 teaspoon water
- 3 cups baby spinach, roughly chopped
- 1 1/2 cups Cremini mushrooms, cleaned and sliced
- Drizzle olive oil
- 6 large eggs
- 1/3 cup milk
- 1/2 teaspoon salt
- 1/4 teaspoon red pepper flakes
- 5 ounces goat cheese, crumbled

Instructions

1. Preheat oven to 400°F. Grease a 10-inch cast-iron skillet with olive oil or cooking spray.
2. In a mixing bowl, stir together the almond meal, garlic, thyme, salt, and pepper. Pour in the olive oil and water and stir until the mixture is thoroughly combined.
3. Press the dough into your prepared skillet/pan until it is evenly dispersed across the bottom and at least 1 1/4 inches up the sides. Bake until the crust is lightly golden and firm to the touch, about 15–20 minutes.
4. In a large skillet over medium heat, warm enough olive oil to lightly coat the pan. Cook the mushrooms with a dash of salt, stirring often, until tender. Toss in the spinach and let it wilt while stirring, about 30 seconds. Transfer the mixture to a plate to cool.
5. In a mixing bowl, whisk together the eggs, milk, salt, and red pepper flakes. Stir in the goat cheese and the slightly cooled mushroom and spinach mixture.
6. Once the crust is done baking, pour in the egg mixture and bake for 30 minutes, or until the center is firm to the touch and cooked through. Let the quiche cool for 5–10 minutes before slicing with a sharp knife.
7. Serve immediately and take all of the credit immediately as well.

BREAKFAST NACHOS

I seriously thought I invented breakfast nachos until I found recipe variations all over the interwebs. Doesn't matter who created them, you and your guy are about to destroy them!

Total Time :20 • Servings: Hahahahaha

Ingredients

- 1/2 pound cooked breakfast sausage (pork, turkey, or plant-based)
- 1 (10-ounce) bag tortilla chips
- 2 cups Monterey Jack cheese, shredded
- 1 cup cheddar cheese, shredded
- 6 eggs
- Salt and pepper
- 1/4 cup of your guy's favorite salsa
- 1 avocado, diced
- 1 cup cherry tomatoes, sliced
- 1/3 cup sour cream
- Garnish: Scallions, pico de gallo, lime wedges, store-bought guacamole, you name it!

Instructions

1. Preheat oven to 375°F.
2. Spread the tortilla chips onto a parchment paper–lined baking sheet.
3. Cover the chips with the shredded cheese and the cooked breakfast sausage.
4. Make 6 little wells in the chips and crack an egg into each one. Sprinkle salt and pepper over the top.
5. Place the baking sheet into the oven on the lowest rack. Bake until the egg whites are cooked through and the yolks are to your desired doneness, about 15 minutes.
6. Remove from oven.
7. Add more cheese to the top because, cheese!
8. Drizzle your favorite salsa over the top of the nachos and top with the diced avocado and cherry tomatoes.
9. Top with the sour cream and any garnishes you desire: scallions, guacamole, whatever makes your day.
10. Serve immediately with more guacamole and taco sauce!
11. Remember to send Wendy Miller a thank-you note.

DUTCH DUTCH BABY

If a pancake and a popover had a baby it would be all over the tabloids. It would also be this dish. I love serving it right out of my cast-iron skillet, because not only is it rustically impressive, but it also means fewer dishes to clean. #Priorities

Total Time :45 • Servings: Ummmm, yeah, *your* call

Ingredients

- 1/2 cup all-purpose flour
- 1/2 cup whole milk
- 2 large eggs
- 2 tablespoons granulated sugar
- 1 teaspoon vanilla extract
- 1/2 teaspoon fine salt
- 2 tablespoons unsalted butter
- Powdered sugar and maple syrup for serving

Instructions

1. Place the flour, milk, eggs, sugar, vanilla, and salt in a blender. Blend for 10 seconds, scrape down the sides, and then blend for another 10 seconds. The batter will be quite liquidy.
2. Leave the batter in the blender and set aside to rest for 20–25 minutes. This gives the flour time to absorb the liquid.
3. Place a 9-inch cast-iron skillet on a middle rack to warm along with the oven.
4. Heat the oven to 425°F.
5. When ready to make the pancake, remove the skillet from the oven using oven mitts and place it on top of the stove. Add the butter and swirl the pan to melt the butter so it coats the bottom and sides of the pan.
6. Pour the batter on top of the butter. Tilt the pan if needed so that the batter runs evenly up all sides. Place the skillet in the oven.
7. Bake until the Dutch baby is puffed, lightly browned across the top, and darker brown on the sides and edges, approximately 15–20 minutes.
8. Leave in pan to serve.
9. Dust with powdered sugar.
10. Cut into wedges and serve with maple syrup.
11. Know that you are a total breakfast badass.

Note: If you want to add fresh fruits such as berries or sliced peaches, put them in the skillet before you add the batter. Otherwise, the fruits might prevent the pancake from rising as high.

DESSERTS
THE "OTHER" KIND OF HAPPY ENDING

They say the way to a man's heart is through his stomach.
Obviously "they" never took
an anatomy class.

Here are a few tried-and-true dessert recipes that will totally
melt your guy's heart—which is also anatomically impossible.

Doesn't matter, I stole my husband's heart years ago. Okay,
that's also not anatomically possible.

Heart idioms are dumb.

TOTES YUMMY BANANA BREAD

Okay, why would I suggest a recipe if it wasn't totally yummy? Well, I actually wanted to call it Totes Yummy and Moist Banana Bread, but a lot of people have a visceral reaction to the word *moist*. Sorry *moist* haters, but this banana bread is MOIST and also totes yummy. Feel free to add chocolate chips or nuts to this recipe. We don't like either in our banana bread. Shut up, we're *not* weirdos. Okay, yeah, we totally are. Whatevs.

Total Time 1:20 • Servings: I'm not even going to dignify that with an answer

Ingredients

- 2 cups all-purpose flour
- 1 teaspoon baking soda
- 1/4 teaspoon salt
- 1/2 cup butter
- 3/4 cup brown sugar
- 2 eggs, beaten
- 2 1/3 cups overripe bananas, mashed

Instructions

1. Preheat oven to 350°F.
2. Lightly grease a 9x5-inch loaf pan.
3. In a large bowl, combine flour, baking soda, and salt.
4. In a separate bowl, cream together butter and brown sugar. Stir in eggs and mashed bananas until well blended.
5. Stir banana mixture into flour mixture; stir just to moisten. Do not overmix.
6. Pour batter into prepared loaf pan.
7. Bake for 60–65 minutes, until a toothpick inserted into center of the loaf comes out clean.
8. Let bread cool in pan for 10 minutes, then turn out onto a wire rack.
9. Slice a piece and bring it to your guy in bed. There's a good chance he will love you forever and everer.

Bonus Suggestion: Use banana bread to make French toast. OMFG you are welcome.

PALEO CHOCOLATE CHIP COOKIES

Whenever I'm baking these around people who can eat all of the gluten they want, I really play up the vegan and gluten free angle so they won't touch them. That works out great for me because these cookies are rich, melty and amazeballs.

Total Time: 2:17 • Servings: There is no such concept as "servings" when it comes to cookies

Ingredients

- 2 cups almond meal
- 1/4 cup arrowroot flour
- 1/2 cup coconut sugar
- 1/4 teaspoon sea salt
- 1/4 teaspoon baking soda
- 1/2 cup palm shortening (I like Spectrum Organic)
- 1 teaspoon vanilla
- 2 tablespoons water
- 1/2 cup chocolate chips

Instructions

1. In a stand mixer with a paddle attachment, mix together dry ingredients.
2. Add the remaining ingredients without the chips and mix together well.
3. Then mix in chips.
4. Scoop into 1 1/2-inch balls on a cookie sheet lined with parchment paper and freeze until they are hard.
5. Only bake frozen dough. Never defrost.
6. Bake frozen cookie dough at 325°F for 17 minutes only. They might look soft, which is fine.
7. Remove from oven and cool on a wire rack. They will harden.
8. Do not overbake.
9. His brain will think these are buttery chocolate chip cookies, but there's no animal fat anywhere to be found. Shhhh, don't tell his brain.

SUPER SIMPLE SNACKS

We were at the wedding of our friends Nikki and Gary. During their exchange of vows, Nikki said, "I promise I will always give you snacks." However, it was a very large outdoor venue, and they weren't wearing microphones, so a lot of us thought she said, "I promise I will always give you sex."

Nikki and Gary have been married for a long time so whatever she's giving him is working.

Each of these snacks isn't exactly a recipe, it's more of a gesture. My husband and I like to do little things for each other to make the other one feel special. One of those things is bringing him snacks while he's watching a movie, working at his desk, or lying in bed wondering where the hell I am. I'll tell you exactly where the hell I am, I'm making him some gott damn snacks!

Sliced Apples and Peanut Butter
We have one of those nifty apple slicers that cores the apple while making 8 perfectly even slices. I'm actually terrified of it, in the same way a dog might be afraid of the vacuum. Actually, I'm also afraid of the vacuum. But I push through my fear and use this gizmo to slice fresh apples for my husband.

Then I arrange the slices nicely around the edge of a plate, and in the middle of the plate I place a dollop of his favorite nut butter. A blob? A mass? Whatever. I place the perfect amount for dipping so he can enjoy just the right amount with every apple slice. He's a Virgo, he likes order. We often share this snack in bed and make sure that each one gets exactly as much as they'd like. That's what makes a happy marriage: letting your partner have the last bite of apple and peanut butter. That and an iron-clad prenup.

Guacamole Deviled Eggs
This is something my husband used to make for me all the time. Until he discovered that mine taste better than his. Now I'm the one who has to make them. What have we learned? If you're a good cook, keep it to yourself. These are actually super simple to prepare and a great low-carb snack. Hard boil 4 eggs. Slice them lengthwise. Remove the yolks and put them in a mixing bowl. Add in a little yellow mustard, a little mayonnaise, and a few scoops of premade guacamole or mashed fresh avocado. Mix it all together and then spoon the mixture into the empty hard-boiled egg halves. Add a little Trader Joe's Chili Lime Seasoning on top and you're on the way to Snack Town. No, I'm not making any money off of Trader Joe's. Eat immediately or refrigerate in a really nifty covered deviled egg carrying case, which I am also not getting paid to recommend.

Popcorn
I don't want to brag but I make the greatest popcorn in the history of ever. You need to keep it very simple and never, ever, buy microwave popcorn. That shit is garbage, and many can be unhealthy. I prefer yellow popping corn because it's sturdier than white and pops bigger. Yes, I am a popcorn size queen.

I pop my popcorn with coconut oil using a stovetop popcorn popper. I drizzle on melted butter and salt in the middle and on top. Don't overthink this. There's something really special about cuddling next to your boo with a big bowl of hot, fresh, buttery popcorn and watching whatever dumb crap he's recorded on your DVR. Cause in about 7 minutes he'll be fast asleep and then you get to put on whatever you want to watch and eat all of the popcorn yourself. That's 32 years of marriage right there.

FUN FOOD FACTS 8

German Chocolate Cake has nothing whatsoever
to do with the country of Germany.

It was named after Sam German,
the guy who created the chocolate.

Totally true!

SECRET #2 — SEX

Is it really a secret that your partner wants sex?

You'd be surprised how many people do not know this.

HOW TO TAME A WILD PENIS

Newsflash! Dudes love blowjobs. Like seriously. A lot. Many women find blowjobs to be daunting and avoid them because they think they're annoying, they're not good at them, or they're very hard work. After all, "job" is in the title.

First of all, if you want to totally own a guy, you need to up your blowjob game. When you get to the point where you know you can totally destroy him with a blowie, you have won. Trust me on this.

Also, don't think of it as a job. It's really more of an avocation. A Blow Hobby.

Plus, 75% of this game is enthusiasm. No matter what, they're happy you're there. If you act as if you're thrilled to be down there, it's really going to be appreciated. Remember, you're totally in charge here. Everyone wants to be an amazing cook or an amazing dancer or an amazing singer. Penis Taming is just another skill for you to master, and once you do, all of the power is yours!

SLOOOOOOOOOOOW DOWN

Anticipation releases the same amount of dopamine as actual pleasure. Meaning, taking your time teasing him during the day, sending sexy texts, or leaving notes in his underwear means increasing the total amount of pleasure he receives.

Instead of going right for the gusto, go slooooooow. Kissing, caressing, stroking with your hands, rubbing your body against his body—all of these sensual techniques will prolong his antici-pation and lead to much more pleasure.

Don't think about oral sex as something you *have* to do for him. If you look at it that way, it won't be as fun for either of you. Reframe it as something you know gives him an enormous amount of pleasure. Plus, the better you get at it, the more you're in control.

A slow, enthusiastic tease will go a long way.

LUBE 101

In the following pages, I talk a lot about lube and why you should be using it. I know it might seem as if this entire book is underwritten by the Lube Industrial Complex (LIC), but I swear it isn't. I mean, I certainly wouldn't be against taking their lube-soaked money, but sadly it has not been offered to me. Yet.

Call me, LIC.

I am here to talk about something important, though. Your comfort. A lot of women I encounter at events complain about suffering through painful sex, especially women over 40 whose hormones are decreasing along with their natural ability to self-lubricate. For some reason, these women seem to think that their partners will somehow be offended if they use lube during sex. As if the act of using lube is offensive to penis owners. Also, some women are afraid to buy lube because they fear it will make them look like some sort of sex fiend.

As if there's something wrong with that!!!!

What I say to my sisters is this: You have no problem going out and spending $45 on a lipstick. Just think of lube as lipstick for your vagina. Using lube to make sex more comfortable for you is not some sort of insult to a man. Over time, the skin in your vagina thins and the pain is legitimate. Plus, if you don't use lube and your skin does tear, it can cause a serious infection. Lube is a way to make the sex less painful and more comfortable FOR BOTH OF YOU.

Use it!

There are different kinds of lube, the primary types being oil-based, water-based, and silicone-based.
Oil-based lube has a very slippery quality, but it also has some issues. It's unsafe to use with condoms, as the oil can degrade the latex and create small tears through which sexually transmitted infections or semen can pass.

Because it's more viscous, if used vaginally or in the anus, oil-based lube can also trap bacteria, which can lead to infections such as bacterial vaginosis. You don't want that. If you're looking to have some fun in the water, oil-based lube will stay slicker than others. But it requires more cleanup than other lubricants and is not good with latex and certain toys.

Water-based lube is good for sensitive skin and is much easier to clean up. It won't stain your sheets and washes off easily. However, it tends to dry faster, so you will have to reapply it more often. Always make sure the water-based lube you're using is petrochemical-free, glycerin-free, and paraben-free. Otherwise, it can cause urinary tract infections, especially if you have a delicate ecosystem.

Silicone-based lube is very slippery, typically hypoallergenic, and less likely to cause irritation. It lasts much longer than water-based lubes.

However, make sure you're using it with the right toys. Silicone lube can deteriorate the surface of silicone toys. When this happens, you create tiny fissures where bacteria can grow. Bacteria is not something you want anywhere near your nether bits in general.

A lot of experts, including my friend, noted Vagina Whisperer and OB/GYN to the stars, Dr. Sherry Ross, recommend pure, virgin, unrefined coconut oil as a lube. All-natural, preservative-free, and sold in massive vats at Costco, coconut oil as a sexual lubricant can be especially pleasant for women going through menopause. Not only is it highly moisturizing and naturally antimicrobial and antifungal, coconut oil retains its slickness for a long time and doesn't clump up like other lubes. It can be messy on your sheets, and like any oil-based lube it shouldn't be used with latex condoms or toys. Also, if you're prone to yeast infections, coconut oil has potential to disrupt the pH balance in your vagina. On the plus side, it's way more affordable than any other lube. And the best part is, when you use it, your guy's dick will taste like Hawaii!

Mahalo!

Petroleum jelly may seem like a slippery option, but it's not a good lubricant for sex. It's difficult to clean off of your skin, can stain your bedding, and can take several days to work its way out of your body. It's also incompatible with latex condoms and toys. Plus, because petroleum jelly stays in your body for such a long time, it may attract bacteria and make you prone to an infection. Women who use petroleum jelly in their vaginas are reportedly more at risk for bacterial vaginosis than women who don't use petroleum jelly.

There are also hybrid lubes available. Finding the right one might require a lot of trial and error. But that makes for some really fun trials, and hopefully not too many yucky errors.

Whichever lube you do decide to use, if you want or need lube in order to have comfortable, safe, or healthier sex, you are well within your rights to demand it.

If your guy thinks using lube is somehow a dig on his ability to arouse you, then explain to him that your body may produce less lubricant as a result of hormonal changes, menopause, medication, hydration, or just naturally. Also, what happens inside your vagina is not always about him. If he wants to make your vagina happy, he needs to listen to its owner.

Lube will make sex better and more comfortable for both of you. If he's not cool with that, you should not be cool with him.

BEFRIEND HIS FRENULUM

The frenulum is the little piece of connective tissue on the underside of the penis at the top of the shaft and base of the head. This is a major pleasure zone and your new best friend.

A great blowjob technique is to wrap both of your hands around the base of his shaft and lower your mouth over the head of his penis.

Flick your tongue back and forth over the frenulum while he's inside your mouth. Vary your speed, depth, and pressure to keep him guessing while the pleasure nearly breaks his brain.

Anatomy: It's your friend!

LET HIS BONER DO THE TALKING

There are times when dirty talk is amazing. It's a great way to let someone know you're in the mood or take them to a whole new place while having sex. Checking in occasionally is fine, too. However, sometimes, you need to read a room—or a cock.

While you're orally pleasing him, keep chatter to a minimum. Don't ask for a progress report. Don't ask if he likes what you're doing. That could take him out of his pleasure zone and make him start to feel performance anxiety.

You can tell if he's having a good time just by listening to his breathing. If his penis is jumping and throbbing, he's happy. When something is working, keep doing it. You can always stop if you want to extend the pleasure and go back to it later. Prolonging pleasure is fun. This isn't a race, so don't be focused on the goal line. Be focused on giving pleasure.

Don't get into your head when you're giving head.

MOUTHWATERING

Spit is not the best lube. It's not even in the top 40. It evaporates quickly and is not very slippery after a few seconds. Plus, depending on your personal diet and other factors, your mouth will eventually dry out. That doesn't mean there's anything wrong with you, it just means you're not a natural lube factory.

For this reason, you can't keep his penis in your mouth the entire time. Not only will that tire out your jaw, the lack of lube can also create discomfort for both parties. Take a break. Have a beverage by the bedside. Play around with different temperatures. Have a glass of cold water by the bedside, or a cup of warm tea (not too hot). After sipping the tea, your mouth will feel nice and warm to him, and that will help increase pleasure and blood flow to the area. You can even hold a little warm tea in your mouth and take him back in it.

You might spill a little bit, but messy sex is fun!

CAN I GET A SHOW OF HANDS?

Your hands are a key part of a great blowjob and also a great way to trick the average penis. As you're licking or sucking on the top of his penis, use your hands to stroke the bottom of the shaft. You can use one hand to lightly massage his balls.

Generously lube up your hands and stroke up and down while he's in your mouth. By partnering your hands with your mouth, you can create one warm and slippery tunnel that will feel as if he's deep inside a vagina. This technique can also give your jaw a chance to rest.

You can also use your hands to stroke his thighs or play with his nipples, if he likes that. A gay friend likes to hold a guy's hand while he's giving head. He says that sends some guys over the edge.

Play with using your hands in all sorts of creative ways. Remember, this is about enthusiasm and gifting your partner with pleasure. So be sure to give him and yourself a hand.

GET DEEP

Don't worry if you have a gag reflex. Most people do. If you want to try deepthroating, here's a technique that might make things a bit easier.

Lie on your back with your head hanging over the edge of the bed. This position naturally elongates your throat. He can slide his penis into your mouth as he stands behind your head. Use your hands to press against his hips—you control how deep he pushes into your throat. As you suck him into your mouth, allow him to increase the depth as you become more relaxed.

Also, this position allows him lots of access to your body if he wants to play with your nipples or run his hand between your legs as he presses into your mouth. This is a great way to try deepthroating, still have control, and get a handie from him at the same time.

Everybody wins!

LOVE CAN BE BLIND

According to Dr. Jessica O'Reilly, author of *The New Sex Bible*, blindfolds are the most popular bedroom prop. "The sensory deprivation you experience when you eliminate the sense of sight only heightens the perception of other senses, making every touch and every whisper all the more titillating."

With your partner's consent, it's easy to play with blindfolds. You don't need to purchase anything special—you can use a scarf or even a sleep mask. Blindfolds can help some people shut out distractions, get out of their head, and magnify pleasure.

Use your hands. Tease him with your mouth. Keep him guessing. This is a fun way to connect with his body on a whole new level, deepen your trust, and advance your creativity in pleasing him.

Help him relax, let go, and surrender completely to you. That's kind of the whole point of this.

THE EYES HAVE IT

This is the exact opposite of the blindfolding technique. Another way to send him over the top is to make eye contact with your partner while he's in your mouth.

This goes back to the enthusiasm piece of all of this. If he knows that you're enjoying pleasing him and that you're there willingly and happily, his pleasure levels will go through the roof. One way to blow a guy's mind while blowing him is to make silent eye contact while you're going down on him.

Men are very sensitive to visual cues, and being able to see your face during a blowjob is a huge turn-on for a lot of guys. It establishes your enthusiasm and is a perfect display of pleasure. It also connects the two of you without a single word being spoken. You don't have to maintain eye contact the entire time, that would be kind of creepy. Plus, sometimes you just want to close your eyes and enjoy giving or receiving pleasure.

But the occasional mindful moment where you can lock eyes with your partner while pleasing him will be a powerful moment for him indeed.

THE TAINT OF HEART

The perineum is a fleshy, highly erogenous area between a man's testicles and butthole. Also known as The Taint, The Chode, The Gooch, and The Road To Happytown, this area may have been neglected by you in the past, but it's really a treasure trove of nerve endings that you need to know better. Not only is the base of the penis located under the skin there, but his prostate is right on the other side of the wall.

It's known as the male G-spot, or more specifically the P-spot, and direct pressure on the perineum can create full-body orgasms.

While you're stroking him or when he's in your mouth, simultaneously reach down there and apply direct pressure by rubbing in a circular motion. Use a side of your finger and not the tip. You don't want to get pointy here. Start out slowly but increase the pressure with his pleasure. You can tell how he's responding based on his breathing and how his penis is responding. Some guys enjoy a vibrator in this area as well.

The prostate gland controls ejaculation. Stimulation to this area not only heightens his sensations and blood flow, it also can lead to harder erections. Plus, studies show that daily ejaculation can reduce the risk of prostate cancer.

Yep, it feels good and it's good for him. This magical spot *taint* to be avoided.

GO NUTS

The scrotum is very sensitive, and like most sensitive things it does not like being ignored.

His testicles are not too sensitive to be touched, they just need to be handled with care. Loaded with nerve endings, you can gently suck on the skin of his scrotal sac. Gently suck a whole ball into your mouth and run your tongue all around it. You can also start at the rear of the perineum and lick all the way up, across his sac, to the tip of his penis. Do this a few times very slowly and he will go nuts. Pun intended.

ON THE OTHER HAND . . .

Maybe you're looking to mix things up a little bit. A lot can be said for a great handjob.

Before you get started, make sure your hands are as soft and smooth as possible. However much lube you think you need, use 30% more. Make sure your nails are free of sharp edges.

If you want to add a fun technique, start by wrapping your hand around his shaft, with your pinky close to his balls. While stroking up and down, rub your thumb over his frenulum. As I mentioned earlier, the frenulum is the little piece of connective tissue on the underside of the penis at the top of the shaft and base of the head. This is a major pleasure zone.

So as you get to the top (with lots of lube, please), rub your thumb back and forth over the frenulum. Then stroke back down. Pay lots of attention to his frenulum as you go over the top of his penis, and that can take him over the top.

THE OVER AND OVER

This technique is fun because it feels constant and rhythmic. And it's kind of like braiding hair, only not at all.

First, apply a large amount of lube. Now a little more. Take your right hand and stroke him from the top of his penis to the bottom. As soon as you reach the bottom, release your hand and make the same stroke, top to bottom with your left hand. Alternate right, left, right, left as if it's one continuous motion, with one hand always sliding on the penis.

This way, he feels endless stroking and you keep alternating hands and the pressure throughout.

Just so you know, you totally need more lube.

AROUND THE COCK

Instead of just stroking his cock up and down, add a fun twist. Slather your hands in lube. Now a little more, and twist as you go up and down. With a small amount of pressure (we're not wringing out a mop here, folks), rotate one hand in a clockwise direction, while rotating the other in a counterclockwise direction.

When you can't twist your hand anymore, reverse the direction and do this twisting move while stroking up and down the shaft. Listen to his breathing. You can ask if he'd like it slower, faster, tighter, or gentler. This is all about providing pleasure to him and knowing that you own him thanks to your badass boner skills.

A NEW TWIST

A very good friend of mine said this is the go-to move of professional sex workers. If anyone knows their way around a boner, it's a professional.

Apply lots of lube to your dominant hand. Now a little more. Grip the erect penis with your palm facing away from you and your thumb pointing down. Firmly grasp at the base of the shaft and slowly slide your hand up towards the head. This may feel a bit awkward, but your palm should still be facing away from you. When you reach the top the penis, twist your hand around the head towards you and as you twist slide your hand off the top. Be sure to pay extra attention to the frenulum as you cross it, because as a penis-pleasing expert you now know that's a super sensitive area.

Grip back at the bottom and repeat. Once you get the rhythm of this move, you can weave the movement between your right and left hands.

Don't worry, you'll get the twist.

A STROKE OF GENIUS

Want to know how a guy likes to be stroked? Have him demonstrate it for you.

Not only is this a very hot and intimate way to play with each other, but he will show you exactly what he likes. Pay attention to the speed. Where he positions his hand. What he does with his other hand. Does he slow down or speed up before reaching orgasm? Watch and learn!

I'm not saying to put on a headlamp and get all Margaret Mead on the guy, but enjoy the show and discover exactly what he likes. Maybe even participate a bit by applying pressure to his perineum with your mouth.

I'm pretty sure he won't get mad at that.

HANDS TOGETHER NOW

Generously lube your hands and his penis. Now add some more lube to both areas.

Wrap both hands around the base of his penis, interlacing your fingers so you create a large ring. Point both of your thumbs upward toward his tip against the underside of his penis. Squeeze and stroke upward, flicking the frenulum with your thumbs as you reach it. Maintain a tight, wet grip as you stroke up and down. Hit the frenulum on every stroke and keep your hands moving.

This will send him into orbit.

PRAY A BIG PART

Rub some of your favorite lube between your palms. You guessed it, add a little bit more. Now warm up your hands and place them in the prayer position.

With your fingers pointing up, lower your hands in the prayer position, over his erect penis. As you get down to the base, open up your index and middle fingers to accommodate his member. Keep those fingers open and slide your hands back up to the tip, slowly returning your hands to the closed prayer position to maintain even pressure. As you cross his frenulum, you can give it a gentle flick with your thumbs.

Lather, rinse, repeat.

Remember, with all hand play, make sure your nails are free of any sharp edges. This is very sensitive tissue and you want to play safe.

OKAY BY HIM

Sometimes less is more. In this case, you'll be using two fingers instead of an entire grasp. The results will be better than okay.

Add a good amount of lube to the penis. Now add some more.

With both hands, use your index finger and thumbs to make two okay signs. Place your okay signs at the base of his shaft. Working together, slide the "rings" up his shaft and over the head and then back down again. Alternate your stroking patterns and twist each okay sign in the opposite direction.

You can also suck on the head of the penis while you do this move for extra credit. Don't worry, this is one class you'll never fail.

IT'S THE LITTLE THINGS

Now that you've taken your boner-friendly techniques to the next level, it's time to think about what else you can bring into the bedroom to increase the pleasure for both of you.

Sometimes it's all in the attitude.

SHE'S A VERY KINKY GIRL . . .

You might be thinking to yourself, "Oh, I'd better not act as if I like sex or he's going to think I'm some kind of perv." Guess what, your guy WANTS you to be a superfreaky perv.

Probably.

If he doesn't want you to reveal the completely natural and crazy, sexy, cool side of you, well, you might want to find another guy who's worthy of your freakiness. Fuck shame!

Or at least don't fuck someone who shames you for wanting to have fun in bed.

You deserve someone who is into all of you and your freakiness with no judgment, okurrrr?

CONFIDENCE CAN GET YOU VERY FAR

Being comfortable in your skin and confident in the bedroom is a HUGE turn-on. For you and him. Be proud and unapologetic about what you like, how you look, and what you need.

If you're worried about what he might say if you want to talk dirty or try toys, then maybe you're not with the right guy. Or maybe he's dealing with his own shame issues and needs to work through them first.

Because we're all raised with so much shame and judgment about sex, women are reluctant to share what we really want in bed because we're afraid men might not respect us or they might be threatened. But a lot of guys really want that freaky part of you to come out. In this changing world, many are afraid to ask for it.

I'm not suggesting you should just spring stuff on him, but it's fun to share fantasies in a neutral, non-bedroom location. Tell him that you want to try toys or restraints or dirty talk or costumes, whatever you're into that's consensual. You might be surprised by how he responds, and you just might find that you get everything you want. Just ask.

CONSENT

Sexual Power Play refers to the very popular (50 Shades . . . hello!) BDSM practice of dominance and submission. This type of play is often misunderstood as abuse of control, but at the center of this dynamic are advanced levels of communication, trust, consent, and aftercare. It is about exploring the boundaries of pleasure in a safe and consensual way, and it can be healing for many.

Okay, cool. So, ummm, what is consent?

Consent is an agreement between participants to engage in sexual activity. Consent must be clearly and freely communicated so that you and your partner(s) understand and respect each other's boundaries.

CONSENT CAN BE REVOKED AT ANY TIME AND FOR ANY REASON.

NO MEANS NO.

You are allowed to change your mind whenever you wish for any reason whatsoever. You are not required to engage in anything you do not wish to do. Even after you've started doing something that you said you were okay with and then while doing it you changed your mind, you are 100% allowed to STOP AT ANY TIME, FOR ANY REASON.

Also, consent cannot be given by individuals who are underage, intoxicated, incapacitated by drugs or alcohol, asleep, or unconscious. If someone tries to force you to engage in an activity under pressure of intimidation or threat, that is not considered consent because it was not given freely.

Once you and your partner agree to the rules of consent, you can start communicating with each other about what types of play you'd like to explore. Take baby steps. First talk about some of the ideas you'd like to explore. Do some research. Then maybe watch a few movies together to decide what kinds of scenes you'd like to create. Feel free to reach out to an expert such as a professional dominatrix or sex therapist to help you navigate the process.

If any experts are judgmental about your new interests, find a more sex-positive one. BDSM and power play can take your relationship to the next level. It isn't all about restraints and pain; there are many layers, and it's a fantastic way to advance your communication and trust skills.

Fun Fact: In a recent study of 1,300 adults, the most popular safe words were *Red*, *Pineapple*, *Banana*, *Orange*, *Peach*, and *Apple*. On my Playboy TV show *Swing*, a very popular couple named Nikki and Daniel had *Onomatopoeia* as their safe word.

Hey, you do you . . . but only with full consent.

DO ASK, DO TELL

I hate to be the one to break this to you, but it turns out, that guy in the bed next to you is not a mind reader. For some misguided reason, many women expect their male partners to somehow know exactly what they're thinking at all times, and then completely resent having to explain anything to them.

Ladies, I'm going to solve a lot of your problems right now. Believe me when I tell you: DUDES DO NOT KNOW WHAT YOU'RE THINKING. LIKE, EVER. They barely know how to load the dishwasher.

You cannot expect your partner to magically know *what* you want, *why* you want it, or *why* you're upset. You have to woman-up and tell his dumb ass. Being angry about this is unfair. You want him to know why you're pissed off without actually telling him because he's the one who may have pissed you off. That is entirely unfair and unrealistic. Also, he doesn't fucking know!

YOU HAVE TO EXPLAIN THINGS TO THESE PEOPLE, THEY ARE VERY BASIC.

Your unexpressed thoughts and wishes are exactly that. Unexpressed. You need to tell your partner exactly what you want, why you are upset, or how they can please you in the manner you desire. Or you can walk around enraged all the time and then nobody's getting laid.

Most people want to be a great partner, and just about everyone wants to be a total Sex God. If you empower your partner by telling them exactly what you want, and when you want it, you are not crushing their fragile ego. You are empowering them to stop doing stupid shit and/or be a Sex God. YOUR Sex God. Do you get what I'm saying here? Communicate *exactly* what you want. Frame it so they know you're giving them the keys to your naughty kingdom. Then get ready for all of the pleasure you can handle.

And a properly loaded dishwasher.

Whether it's about sex or the everyday drama of life, once you get to the point where you can communicate clearly and directly without assigning meaning to their actions (which they know nothing about), you can take your relationship to a whole new level. Look, men are hella basic, but women are over-wired. This pairing is challenging. It's like trying to fix a BMW with a spork.

There is middle ground. We need to accept each other for who we are, as we are. Be honest, direct, fair, non-accusatory, and clear in your communication.

Also, in the grand scheme of things, it doesn't fucking matter how the dishwasher is loaded.

I mean, really.

SEXYTIME STUFF!

I'm a big fan of sex toys and adult products. They can enhance your play and really add some extra fun to the bedroom.

As a general rule, I strongly suggest you don't surprise your guy and bring anything penis-shaped into the bed that's larger than your guy's actual penis. They can be touchy about that stuff. At least when you first start playing with sex toys. You'll have to trust me on this.

The following are everyday items that happen to be great at enhancing sex play. All are easy to find, and I think they can really add some heat to your bedroom . . . or living room . . . or that icky corner of the basement by the hot water heater.

You know what I mean.

PEARLS

Author and noted sex educator Lou Paget, has for years been extolling the virtues of pearls during oral sex with penis owners. If you have a longer strand of well-made fake pearls, wear them all day so your body warms them up. You'll be the fanciest person in the laundromat.

Then later, when you're ready to have some fun, take off the fake pearls and cover them generously with lube. Coil the pearls around the shaft of your partner's penis comfortably but snug enough so that the beads are rested against him. Intertwine your fingers and place the palms of your hands on either side of his penis. Then, slide your hands up and down in a wave motion, causing the warm, lubed beads to roll up and down his shaft.

Do this correctly and you'll have a brand-new pearl necklace in minutes.

A YOGA BALL

The yoga ball, also known as a gym ball, exercise ball, stability ball, or impulse purchase constantly mocking you from the corner of your home office, is a large, inflatable ball that's fantastic for sex, since you can position yourself all over it for extra stability, and they give you a really nice bounce.

Plus, everyone who sees it in your house will think you're doing a serious core workout when, in actuality, you're using it for boning.

Hey, they're practically the same thing anyway.

WAX ON, GET OFF

I am not suggesting that you insert any candle into any orifices. EVER. But sex by candlelight and/or hot wax play can be very fun, and if you're cheap like me, you have a whole cabinet full of random dollar store candles you've planned on using for a huge romantic gesture you haven't gotten around to yet.

Of course, whenever you use a candle, make sure the area is free of flammable items. Be mindful of your lingerie and bedding as well. Try to use body-safe candles made of soy or paraffin. Beeswax candles burn very hot and can singe your skin. Always play safely. Also, when wax cools and hardens it can be very painful to remove from areas with body hair. Like a Band-Aid times 1,000,000. You can shave the areas ahead of time. Some folks like to prep the areas with baby oil, which can make the wax removal much easier.

This can be really hot. Literally.

GOOD VIBES ALL AROUND

News Flash! Vibrators are not just for women. Men can derive a lot of pleasure from vibrations on their bodies as well. But, before you pull out your battery-operated bestie, keep a few things in mind. Some straight men may regard sex toys exclusively as lady-products. Those are typically men who haven't tried one yet. Regardless, you need to be aware of this possible stigma, and never, ever introduce a vibrator without getting full consent first. Don't just whip out your Buzz-O-Matic 9000 and expect a straight male partner to be thrilled. Also, for obvious reasons, I would recommend you do not use a vibrator that resembles a gigantic penis. Have something more gender-neutral on hand for your favorite fella. Maybe something with a manly camo print or NASCAR branding all over it.

Gentlemen, start your engines!

This is all about pleasure. Slowly introduce the vibrator to his nipples and work your way down. Every person is different.

He may enjoy direct pressure on his shaft, frenulum or directly against his perineum, adjacent to his prostate. He might ask you to add the pressure while he's stroking himself or he might want to lie back and let you and a vibrator take full control.

Be patient. Be gentle at first, and remember, this is about giving him pleasure, not your ego. You never know, next time you might both be reaching for a battery operated bestie.

FIT TO BE TIED UP

These are items you likely have lying around your house in great abundance, and they are excellent for DIY light bondage and blindfold play. Seriously, you don't need one of those fancy pink pleather bondage kits with a contorted adult performer on the box. Don't buy—DIY! Just make sure that your knots aren't too tight. You don't want to cut off circulation.

Also, never use an Hermès scarf for BDSM. Unless you're fucking Grace Kelly.

THE SECRET LIFE OF SCRUNCHIES

You probably don't know this, but the scrunchie was patented in 1987 by nightclub singer Rommy Revson, who once opened for Frank Sinatra. She wanted to create an elastic tie that didn't damage her hair. She created a legacy!

It turns out, the scrunchie can also be great as a cock ring. It's suggested you place the scrunchie around his entire package, looping around and under his balls. Please make sure this is not too tight, or you can cause damage. To him. Or to the scrunchie, I suppose. A well-placed cock ring makes the penis tissue harder and slightly bigger for a longer period of time. It can also delay orgasm, which may result in a much more intense happy ending.

Pro Tip: Don't grab the first scrunchie you see at the mall. Many penis owners might object to having something frilly or princess–themed wrapped around their junk. They're funny that way.

Always be mindful of the scrunchie end user.

PLASTICS!

One of my favorite sex products is a vapor barrier sex blanket. It's covered in black velvet and looks as if it's some fancy bed throw when, in actuality, it's purpose-built for boning. I love stealth sex stuff!

But you don't have to spend upwards of $100 on a fancy sex blanket like mine. Probably somewhere in your kitchen, bathroom, or garage you have clean, waterproof sheeting of some sort. A shower curtain liner, a cheap plastic tablecloth, or plastic painting tarp will do the trick. Go crazy! Throw that stuff over your bed and try all sorts of messy stuff. Once you lay down a vapor barrier, your sheets and bedding will remain pristine. If you choose to cover your guy with chocolate hazelnut spread, whipped cream, or anything else sticky or sweet, please remember that many foods can cause some real issues with your lady parts. The sugars can irritate your skin and seriously disturb your natural bacteria, which can lead to an infection, which is not sexy at all.

Remember, you want F-U-N, not a U-T-I.

BUZZZZZZ-ANG!

You want to have some serious fun? Purchase one of my all-time favorite sex toys: a remote-controlled vibrator.

You place the vibe in your underwear against your naughty bits and then give the controller to your guy. Then, maybe choose a romantic restaurant. Throughout the night, your partner gets to zap you with the vibrator. Short time, long time, pulsing, staccato—you never know what's coming . . . except *hopefully* you.

This is one of my all-time favorite toys and a really fun way to warm up before you get home. Just a word of warning: don't use it in a quiet location. This toy can be somewhat audible, and you don't want the people seated next to you at the sushi bar to hear the buzzing going on in your underwear.

Unless you do.

A NAUGHTY VAULT

I'm a big fan of sex toys, high-end lube, and any products that make sex even more fun. But where to keep them? Your nightstand drawer? Good luck if you have snoopy kids or an overzealous housekeeper. Keep everything in a box on the top shelf of your closet? "Don't move, honey, I'll be right back in 25 minutes." Vibe killed.

What you need in your sex sanctuary is a naughty vault -- a small, locking box so everything you need is right within reach. And locked up. When you're done, clean your toys (see next chapter), dry them, slam, click, and slide it back under the bed. It's locked to keep everyone out except you. There are several really great locking vaults that can fit right under your bed or in a nightstand drawer.

They come in a bunch of fun colors and no one will ever know it's there. And if they do, it's locked. Just remember to keep everything fully charged and cleaned in advance so it's ready when you are.

KEEP IT CLEAN WHEN YOU'RE GETTING DIRTY

You're in the throes of passion. Looking to add a whole new level to your pleasure, you want your favorite sex toy. Maybe there are kids in the house or nosey roommates, so you keep your playthings stashed away behind those pants you'll never fit into on the top shelf of your closet. Your partner goes hunting for it, they're taking a long time, with every second you're losing your mojo. They can't find it. They're yelling for you from the closet. Where is it?!?! You're getting angry and now NOBODY is going to have an orgasm.

GAHHHHH!

Orrrrrr, you think you're slick and you keep your favorite items in your yucky nightstand drawer. Annnnd, you're probably not washing it after every use, but who cares, it's just you using it and it's totally fine in there, right?

Uh, no.

That drawer is filled with used hair ties, old Starbucks cards, throat lozenges, a backstage pass from a Duran Duran concert, sunglasses, coupons, and a thick layer of dust, germs, and crust.

THIS IS NOT CUTE, and you are asking for all sorts of trouble such as yeast infections, UTIs, and bacterial vaginosis if you're not cleaning and storing your pleasure products correctly.

You don't have to get super fancy; you can clean your sex toys with good old soap and hot water. Add a drop or two to your item, give it a good massage, and then rinse with water. Air drying is safer than using a towel, which may create cross-contamination. If you have sensitive skin, use an unscented soap. There are spray cleaners, UV light sanitizers, foaming cleaners, wipes—the bottom line is there are options, and you should be using at least one of them on the regular.

If your toys are non-motorized and made of medical-grade silicone, stainless steel, or glass, they may be able to be cleaned in your dishwasher on the top rack (check with manufacturer first). Just make sure your roomies and/or other residents of the house are cool with you placing your sex toys in the dishwasher. The last thing you want is someone reaching in for a coffee mug and instead finding a Vajjbuster 4000.

Always wash brand-new items before using them, and check with the manufacturer of motorized products for cleaning best practices.

It's fine to get dirty, as long as you keep it clean.

ADVENTURES

GREAT SEX DOESN'T ALWAYS BEGIN IN THE BEDROOM

Planning sexy adventures outside the home is a great way to keep your sex life sizzling, and you get to have a lot of naughty fun. The following field trips and ridiculous ideas may, or may not, have been personally attempted by my husband and me.

Either way, have fun!

VISIT YOUR LOCAL SEX SHOP

Despite the blacked-out windows, please don't be afraid to enter these establishments. Many are safe, feminist-owned, and pretty darn nice inside.

I went to one sex toy shop in LA that was like the Barneys of butt plugs. Ya know, if Barneys actually sold butt plugs, they might still be open.

Seriously, I promise you, going to a sex toy shop can be a really fun outing for you and your boo, and a great way to add some excitement for what . . . or *who* . . . is about to come later. Walk around together, look at the fun stuff, maybe share a few fantasies, and then either pick out a few toys together or separate and surprise each other with a fun toy. This way, instead of freaking a guy out when you ambush him with a 16-inch dildo one night, you get immediate buy-in if he personally selects some items. Be open-minded and have some damn fun!

They're called sex TOYS for a reason.

GET SOME CLASS!

Many of the larger, established adult toy shops offer sex technique classes, and often they're free. This is a great way to up your sex game and then use these sex skills on each other later. If you don't live near an establishment that offers sexual technique classes, check out several that are available online. Many of the classes are available for free.

Get your learn on and your turn on.

MOTEL HELL-O!

Want a romantic getaway with free HBO, parking, AND a fancy sheet of paper over the toilet seat that says *Sanitized For Your Protection*? Who doesn't! That, my friends, is why a sleazy road-side motel is a thing of mid-century greatness and perfect for a night of sexy, low-rent fun.

Everybody knows that hotel sex is hot, but banging in a cheap motel takes things to a whole new level. I suggest you create an entire Low Budget Theme Night. Instead of dining on Beef Wellington, chocolate-dipped strawberries, and champagne at the Ritz, bring in some Popeye's, a dozen cannoli, and a fine box of Franzia to the Astro Motel. A boxed Chardonnay pairs quite nicely with a 3-piece.

Why not take the entire thing to performance-art levels? Check in wearing your favorite trashy clothes with a Hefty bag as your luggage.

Many wonder: What Would Jesus Do? I wonder: What Would John Waters Do?

Read online reviews of local no-tell motels. Many of the reviews are accidentally hilarious.

Choose your motel, check in, Lysol the crap out of your room, and have fun! If you're germ/pest-phobic, cover the entire bed with a huge plastic tarp from the hardware store. Enjoy your majestic feast in bed, turn on the in-room smut, and have a fantastic time right on the tarp.

Pro Tip: Leave the tarp. Take the cannoli.

NAKED DAY!

This idea actually came from one of my very best friends and a regular listener of my podcast, *Sex Ed The Musical*.

Her daughter was away for the weekend, so she and her husband decided to spend the entire day together totally naked. She said it was an incredible time and they had tons of fun . . . and sex. 'Cause when you're naked, that's kinda what happens.

Obviously, you need to stay home to do this, but if you live in a nudist resort you can be a total renegade and walk around wearing pants.

That'll show 'em!

DON'T DO THIS, WHATEVER YOU DO

One thing you should know about me is that I am obsessed with shopping for real estate. I blame the countless hours of house-hunting shows I hatewatch on TV and the many open houses I attend for no reason at all.

Just know that I am NOT suggesting that you have a quickie in an open house. Despite how fun it sounds to sneak into a bathroom with your partner and have sex while people are walking through a reimagined modern farmhouse with wide-plank oak floors and a subway tile backsplash, I am absolutely not suggesting you have sex in it. Especially since you can't hide anything behind those stupid barn doors that everyone will be replacing in three years.

I am not at all suggesting that you find a spot behind a door that locks and have a quickie standing up right there, because that is against the law and you can get arrested. No way would I ever recommend you do that, because there is nothing sexy about almost getting caught. So I'm not recommending that at all.

Definitely do not have sex at an open house this weekend, especially right before they're about to close and almost no one is there.

Nope.

Don't do that.

ROOM WITH A SCREW

It's good to set goals, right? So this weekend, you and your partner should set the lofty goal to have sex in every single room of your house. In one night.

Furniture, floors, against your IKEA bookcases. This might be simple if you live in a 210-square-foot Brooklyn apartment that rents for $5,000 a month. But if you live in a sprawling mansion, please stay hydrated.

This is a great couples goal and lots of fun. Plus, after banging on it, you'll never look at your Brazilian cherry-inspired porcelain tile kitchen floor the same way again.

Also, when you're doing the horizontal mambo on your clothes dryer, you'll probably find that earring you lost.

Sin/win!

ROLEPLAYING!

One super fun activity you can try this weekend is going to a local bar alone . . . ish. One of you walks into the bar and orders a drink. The other takes a few minutes and then enters and tries to pick you up. This is a really fun way to roleplay. You can create all-new characters for yourselves. Groovy jobs, new backstories—see how far you both can take it. Stay in character the entire time and really have some fun with this. Extra points if it's a hotel bar so you can go right upstairs and have hotel sex.

Pro Tip: Make sure the one doing the picking up has already checked into the room. You don't want to play this entire game and then have it all cool off while Savannah L. at the front desk is taking her sweet time finding you a non-smoking standard deluxe premium courtyard-view room. So get that shit locked down in advance.

Extra points if one of you calls yourself Mr. Gladstone.

BE AROUND OTHER NAKED PEOPLE

If you're looking for a sexy thing to do this weekend, go to a sex club or a sex party.

If you live in a big-ish city, there's probably an active swinging lifestyle or sex party scene nearby. The best part of attending these parties is you can be inspired by others around you—and you never have to do a thing with anyone. Many sex club visitors and people in the lifestyle typically follow very clear rules of consent. In fact, you're probably a lot safer at a sex club than you are at a regular bar, or truck stop gloryhole. Listen to Episode 35 of my podcast, *Sex Ed The Musical*, that tells you everything you need to know about attending a sex party and establishing your rules in advance. It's a great way to get your communication game on point.

Search online for parties or clubs near you. Always be safe. Be sure to communicate and agree to all of your rules with your partner in advance.

Then go.

And remember, **no audibles once you're there**.

No matter how sexy and fun things appear, and how many hotties hit on you, if it's not part of your previously agreed-upon game plan, then it's off the table.

Don't deviate from the rules you set before arriving.

As I like to say, "Never try to renegotiate in the middle of an orgy. Or you are in for a very tense ride home."

Maybe worse.

If you want to experience a sex party, you and your partner need to agree on all of your rules in advance. If something you didn't discuss happens to come up, walk away.

If there's one place where people know how to respect rules, it's usually a sex party.

FUN WITH YOUR CLOTHES ON

Your pre-gaming doesn't always have to include sex. The truth is, just spending time with your partner doing anything fun is a great way to connect . . . which leads to boning later.

Not too long ago, my husband and I went axe-throwing. We're definitely not lumberjack types, but let me say this much: for a couple of dazzling urbanites in a rustic setting, we did pretty well. Also, seeing my husband throwing an axe like a boss was hella hot. He looked like a Black Brawny paper towels guy. HOTTTT!

There are so many unique and fun things you can do together. Take a salsa class at a local ballroom dance studio. Try an escape room or a candlelit painting class. Go bowling. It doesn't have to be elaborate, it doesn't have to be impressive, it just has to be something fun you can do together.

This is how to stay connected, which leads to the fun naked stuff later.

DIRTY TALK

Dirty talk is something that scares a lot of people. The talkers more than the talkees. Because you're really putting yourself out there and you don't know how your partner will react. Also, you might be concerned that being overtly sexual might freak a guy out. Plus, no one wants to feel like a weirdo when they're naked.

I have a friend whose husband kept begging her to talk dirty in bed and she refused. Until one night he begged her endlessly, so she yelled, "You're a fucking asshole and I hate you."

Fun Fact: They are now divorced.

Anyway, talking dirty in bed can be a lot of fun, and if you want to try it, start out slowly. Instead of channeling your inner super-freak, you can simply describe what you're doing. Tell him what you're going to do. Tell him how it feels for you. How their body is reacting. How turned on they're getting. Straightforward stuff.

Also, use their name. "Oh, Shadrack, I love when you do this to me." Of course, this only works if you're banging someone named Shadrack. Always make sure you use the right name, or at least the name they gave you.

Someone once called me by his ex-girlfriend's name during sex. When I got upset, he told me she was hotter than me so it was a compliment.

Honestly, I don't know what to do with these people sometimes.

Anyway, don't think you have to put yourself out there and be a super perv from the jump. Work your way up to total pervness. Start small. If power play is interesting to you, work your way up to commands. Some guys love being told exactly what to do, especially if you can assert some real authority. Authority when you're naked is very, very sexy.

If you're shy, just throw out a few compliments. I love the way you do that . . . you're so freakin' hot . . . you taste amazing . . . A few words will go a long way and really enhance your fun in bed.

You can totally do this.

FUCK SHUI

We dream all day long about remodeling our kitchens and bathrooms and creating a fantasy backyard, and when I say "we" I mean me. But what about the one room in the house where you spend more time than anywhere else? The room that's supposed to be your private sanctuary. The room where your most important intimate time is spent. You know, the room that's probably overloaded with mismatched bedding, unfolded laundry, pictures of your family, stuffed animals, unfinished projects, stacks of books, last year's tax returns, and a dresser covered in ATM receipts.

YUCK!

Here's a sad but true fact: If your master bedroom has lost its mojo, there's a good chance your relationship is next.

But do not despair, because I am obsessed with two things: Interior Design and Better Sex. These simple changes will add some serious FUCK SHUI™ to your bedroom. Let's get it on!

GET A DAMN LOCK!

Your bedroom door needs a lock. Seriously, you need a lock on your door. You just do. A very good friend of mine told me how her husband was once railing her from behind and their ten-year-old son who was half asleep walked right into their bedroom, crawled into the bed they were on, and fell asleep. I asked her what she did, and she said, "Well, we didn't want to wake him up, so we just went to sleep, too."

Boundaries are your friend! Your kids do not need full access to your bedroom day and night. You should explain the concept of private adult time and the importance of respecting each other's privacy. Your kids will not get broken if they're locked out of your bedroom. They can go back into their own damn rooms and leave you two the fuck alone. It's much worse if you stop having sex because you're terrified that little Timmy might walk in and crawl in bed with you. Timmy has his own bed and he'll be fine there.

Get a lock, put it on your door, and use it. All the time. This will increase your sense of safety, which helps you to relax, let go, and reach orgasm.

If you're concerned that you won't be able to install a lock or are worried about drilling into your wall, try a simple portable door lock. They're great for traveling, and we all know how awesome hotel sex is!

This one is a no-brainer, so do it. Put a lock on your bedroom door and you'll unlock all sorts of fun.

TV IS YOUR FRIEND

Now, a lot of my esteemed colleagues may disagree with me and recommend that you absolutely need to get the TV out of the bedroom, but I say otherwise. I love TV. I work in TV. To quote the brilliant Wanda Sykes, "TV paid for the TV."

I'm not removing it from my bedroom anytime soon.

There are lots of sexy things you can watch together, and everyone can benefit from a little video kindling once in a while. I will say that you need to be very mindful to keep notorious boner killers off the screen. So please no watching the news, stock reports, or that gut-wrenching, four-minute ASPCA commercial. 'Cause that thing will murder any boner within a two-hundred-mile radius. *For Just 63 Cents a Day, You Can Help Rescue Animals From Cruelty.* Well great, now no one is getting laid. Thanks for nothing, Sarah McLachlan.

Having a TV in the bedroom is okay, just remember to keep it sexy. Yay, TV!

TURN DOWN THE LIGHTS

Trust me, I've produced hundreds of hours of TV shows featuring sex. Lighting is everything. To properly set the mood in your sex sanctuary, if you only have overhead lights, install a dimmer switch.

When you go to the hardware store to pick up that bedroom lock, pick up a dimmer switch, too. Most light fixtures will work with standard dimmer switches, including those with halogen and incandescent bulbs. If you have LED fixtures in your bedroom, you might need a specialized dimmer. Just ask that helpful guy in the colorful vest who's easy to find at your local big box hardware store. Hahahaha, I'm joking of course. That guy is no help and he's not around anyway. Ask Dr. Google or a professional electrician.

This is an important detail for setting the best possible mood in your sex sanctuary, because **the better the lighting, the better the banging.**

Masters and Johnson actually said that. Laverne Masters and George Johnson, my neighbors.

You may be a sex-in-the-dark type, which is 100% fine. But your bedroom should be all about setting the mood. Always make sure your lighting is on point. Not too harsh. You want to it to be warm and flattering.

You paid $11 for that lingerie at the car wash, you want your partner to see *just the right amount* of it!

THE PICTURE-PERFECT BEDROOM

For the love of all things sexy, please remove the photos of your kids and family from your bedroom. Right fucking now.

Imagine your partner is going down on you, you're in the throes of passion, you look to your left, and there on the nightstand is a photo of your mother-in-law at a luau. (Slide whistle down sound effect).

There are 36,000 photos of your kids, family, and cat all over the house. Please remove all of them from your bedroom. Your parents on a cruise to Jamaica in 1974 is not what you need displayed in your love nest. Your kid's fourth-grade class photo needs to go. Even pictures of your pets need to GTFO.

Anything that can distract you from the task at someone's hand needs to be removed from your bedroom, stat. Your bedroom is an oasis, not a scrapbook. Simple art, one or two romantic photos of the two of you, but nothing else.

Get the picture? Now immediately remove it.

CLUTTER IS A BONER KILLER!

This one is going to be tough, but you really have to get rid of everything in your bedroom that's not conducive to fucking or sleep. What does that mean? Thank you for asking, I will clarify. You need to remove all of that unfolded laundry. Unfinished projects. Stacks of books you will not be reading. Clothes to donate to charity. Old magazines. Crap.

You need to clear off all of the bills, receipts, tax records, phone chargers, and Bed Bath & Beyond coupons strewn all over your nightstand. That vision board you created? Move it to another room. Junk makes noise, and it's distracting. How can you have a killer, full body orgasm when your tax return is within three feet of your head? You can't, that's a scientific fact!

Please clear all distractions, clutter, and kid stuff out of your sex sanctuary. If you have to have a desk in your bedroom, see if you can keep the top free of any clutter and keep your electronics away from the bed. You want to do whatever you can to remove any office-y distractions from your love nest. These are things that you really need to get under control. The "quieter" your bedroom is, the more relaxed you'll feel and the better sex you'll have.

SHEET MUSIC

You don't have to spend a fortune, but you need to make an investment in sexy bedding. All-new sheets, pillowcases, throw pillows, and a duvet cover can wake up your bed. We're talking rich colors and silky, sexy textures. That's why hotel sex is so fun. It's a room free of clutter with really fine bedding. Invest in higher thread count sheets. Get rid of those disgusting old pillows that look like civil war bandages. Get some fun throw pillows and a couple of sex wedges that look like pillows. Stealth sex strikes again!

You're an adult, so get nice adult bedding. Whatever you do, do not spend a third of your life on low thread count sheets. You deserve Egyptian Cotton, bitches!

This one is important. You deserve it!

SOUNDPROOFING

Is your bed on the same wall as another bedroom? Do you want a little extra privacy for when things get a little extra freaky?

There are all sorts of things you can do to help soundproof your bedroom. Think about installing natural cork tiles on the wall, or maybe hang some rich, heavy fabrics behind your bed. Seal the gap under your door by applying self-adhesive weather stripping. Move your bed off of a shared wall with another bedroom. Install special wallpaper that's designed to dampen the sound.

You can install a wall of acoustic foam panels and even paint them to to match your wall color. Keep in mind that paint can clog their open cellular structure, which might diminish some of their sound-dampening quality. Yes, I've spent a lot of time thinking about this. Get creative, there are all sorts of creative ways to make your bedroom more soundproof.

Do it in the name of design, and no one will be the wiser.

SECRET #3 — LEAVE HIM ALONE

Now, some readers might bristle at the suggestion to leave their guy alone.

"I already cooked him fifty meals and did all of the dirty things! What's in this for me!?!"

Girl, this section is 100% for YOU!

Leaving him alone actually means focusing on you. YOU. This is all about self-care, self-improvement, self-growth, and self-love! Ways you can nurture yourself by yourself, master new skills, and level up your awesomeness.

Dudes are ridiculously simple, and you really don't need them around all of the time. Also, if your guy actually *wants* to spend every minute with you in the craft store, you might be looking at a much bigger problem.

Seriously, this section is about realizing now and forever that YOU COME FIRST.

Carve time out for yourself. Take care of yourself. Improve yourself. Empower yourself. Strengthen your pelvic floor. Yep, we're going to go there, too.

Because *that* is the ultimate in self-care.

Okay, enough about him. It's *you* time!

ARE YOU AFRAID OF SOMETHING? DO IT!

Right before my last zero birthday, I took a serious look at my life. I realized that there were a ton of things I had never tried because I was either terrified or I was certain I'd be terrible at them. That's no way to get through life, and it's definitely no way to get better at anything new.

So I went on a scary bender.

I decided ONLY to do things that terrified me or that I assumed I couldn't do.

- I made curtains and hung them in my kitchen. They turned out fine (don't look too closely).
- I took a surfing lesson. I was terrible, but it was fun.
- I tried brussels sprouts. Covered in bacon, they're quite delicious.
- I had all sorts of consensual sexual adventures. Life. Changed.

My point is, you don't have a lot of time on this planet, and facing your fears head-on will teach you a few critical lessons.

- You can accomplish a lot more than you ever believed.
- You're going to get some great stories out of it and really feel proud of yourself.
- Once you tackle them, that scary list gets shorter and shorter.
- Even if things somehow go wrong, you learn something new, which means you still win.
- It's insane to spend your life cowering in fear of things such as brussels sprouts.

Here's what I'm asking you to do. Put together a list of everything that terrifies you, things that you'd never try but are maybe a little curious about. From little things such as never eating arugula or singing in public, to big things such as going white water rafting or exploring a whole new aspect of your sexuality. Then I want you to start knocking shit off of your list like a boss. You will feel empowered. You will feel invincible. You might feel sore (I took a spin class and it broke my vulva for a week). But I did it and the sensation returned eventually.

You don't want to reach the end of your life with a long list of stupid things you somehow allowed to intimidate you. Make that list. Check it twice. Then start checking that shit off. You will come out stronger, prouder, badder, maybe a little sorer, but definitely a lot less afraid.

SEX WITH THE PERSON YOU
LOVE MOST

"Among all types of sexual activity,
masturbation is . . . the one in which
the female most frequently reaches orgasm."
—Alfred C. Kinsey

Menage a moi. Womansplaining yourself. Visiting the Batcave. Dialing the rotary phone.

Even though few women openly discuss their personal DIY time, studies show that 90% of us are rubbing one out on the regular. That means nine out of ten women are doing something right. Because masturbation is not a deviant act. It's actually a revolutionary act against the patriarchy, with genuine health, sex, and beauty benefits.

FACT: You're more likely to reach orgasms during sex with a partner if you know exactly the kind of touch your body needs to get there.

FACT: The more orgasms you have, the more you want.

FACT: Masturbation is a natural stress reliever.

FACT: Orgasms can help strengthen your pelvic floor.

FACT: During menopause, the vagina can narrow, which can make intercourse more painful. But masturbation can help boost blood flow, relieve some tissue and moisture problems, and increase sexual desire.

FACT: Masturbating can release the feel-good hormone oxytocin, which can naturally relieve stress and anxiety and can help you fall asleep.

FACT: Women have no refractory period. We can have as many orgasms as our bodies will allow.

FACT: Masturbation works like mindful meditation. Rubbing one out is a great way to help anchor you in the present moment.

FACT: Shirley Jones, TV's Mrs. Partridge, revealed in her tell-all memoir that her secret for staying so youthful and vibrant is— you guessed it—DAILY MASTURBATION!

Think of masturbation as sex with your best friend. You're nice to your best friend. Do something nice for her every day, and she will return the favor in all sorts of ways.

To Recap: Masturbation is good for you. It feels great. TV's Shirley Partridge does it on the daily and she's a fucking goddess.

Ladies, let's start a revolution, one orgasm at a time! It's the ultimate in self-care.

Masturbation…an orgasm you never have to fake.

TAKE YOURSELF TO THE EDGE

Since we're already besties who talk about masturbation, now I'm going tell you how to take self-pleasure to the next level, or to the edge, to be exact.

There's a technique called edging, where you take yourself just to the edge of orgasm and then stop. Wait a few seconds and start all over again. You might be thinking, *what fresh hell is this?* Well, I'll tell you. It's an awesome kind of fresh hell that will actually lead to much better release when you do have an orgasm, and it will also really enhance your partnered sex.

There's a direct correlation between how much time you spend getting aroused and how strong your orgasms are. Now, sometimes you just want to get off quickly, so you reach for the Vaj-O-Matic 3000 and buzz one off in a few seconds. Fast and convenient, it's like a microwave for your ladyparts. However, unless you're heating up last night's gnocchi Pomodoro with portobello mushrooms, not very many good things come out of a microwave.

If you want to take your pleasure to the next level, prolong it. First of all, anticipation is pleasure, so even when you're delaying your orgasms, you're enjoying an extended amount of pleasure. Second, this is a great way for you to really get in touch with your body and to spend a luxurious amount of time increasing your arousal levels. Instant gratification isn't as pleasurable as getting something you've wanted for a while. The longer you wait, the better the payoff will be.

If you're using a vibrator, take yourself close to the edge of that cliff but stop before you climax. Pause. Take a moment and breathe deeply. Think about how you're doing something very nice for yourself. Let your blood flow ease a bit. Then lather, rinse, repeat.

Edging is a really great way to learn how to control your own arousal and release, to experiment with pressure and speed, and to learn more about your body and how it changes during climax. The more you know about your body, the better you'll be at communicating exactly what you want from your partner in order to have an orgasm.

There are all sorts of ways edging can enhance your pleasure. If you and your partner have regular sex nights, edging is a great way to pre-game. Knowing that nookie is on the calendar, edge yourself a few times during the late afternoon, but don't go over the cliff. Practice restraint. You'll soon discover that by the time you hop in bed/bathroom floor/backyard bounce castle with your partner, your sex drive has become that of a seventeen-year-old boy's—without the requisite stupidity and wet corn chip smell. You're going to be ready for fun from the jump.

It's your body, it's your arousal, and it's your orgasm. **Remember, you are responsible for your own pleasure.** Not your partner. YOU. Edging is a great way to master masturbation.

CHOOSE YOUR WORDS WISELY

Slut. Whore. Trollop. Skank. Nympho. THAT kind of girl. Have you ever noticed how many words there are for judging women who enjoy sex?

Now let's consider some of the words for men who enjoy sex. Gigolo. Stud. Casanova. Player. Ladies' man.

Wait a second! All of those are compliments!

That's weird.

No, it's actually quite deliberate. In fact, if you want to insult a man who likes sex, you have to call him a man whore or a man slut. That's right, you have to call him a name that is reserved for demeaning women.

When it comes to sex, the shackles of shame and morality are locked firmly on the bodies of women. We are the ones who are judged for enjoying sexual pleasure, or "accused" of enjoying sexual pleasure, or told we were "asking to be sexually assaulted" simply by virtue of our clothing choices, alcohol intake, or by daring to be in a parking lot after sundown.

Whether consensual or not, we're told over and over again that sex is definitely not for our enjoyment, it's shameful and dirty and we shouldn't be interested in it. If we are, we're garbage.

Exactly who's controlling that narrative? Certainly a lot of women routinely slut-shame other women. We've all encountered those women, and some of us have been those women. Then there's the omnipresent male gaze to which we all must conform in some way. We're all expected to be friendly, accommodating, hot, sexy, and magazine-cover fuckable at all times. It's gotten to the point where it's an act of defiance to leave your house without wearing makeup. The whole thing is set up precisely so we can't win. And in the age of social media, the shaming is more prevalent, anonymous, and vicious than ever.

Slut-shaming is more than just words, it's an attack on our autonomy. It's a way of controlling women and preventing us from pursuing pleasure. Okay, you might be thinking, "Ugh, this is annoying and maybe it's just easier to keep my mouth shut and play the game. Who cares?" The whole "lady in the living room, whore in the bedroom" thing is pretty harmless, right?

NO, IT'S NOT FUCKING HARMLESS.

At the core of slut-shaming is the entitlement and belief that men are celebrated for asserting themselves sexually and women are not. It's just another way of perpetuating rape culture and controlling and demeaning women. We need to stop participating in this in any way.

Slut-shaming is rooted in patriarchal expectations of women. It's based in preventing women from being sexually liberated because, for many men, that's the most threatening thing there is. The less women are taught about sex and pleasure, the worse men can be at providing it. Once a woman is empowered and knows what's what, men can be seriously threatened.

The truth is, this isn't 1850, and there's a pretty good chance you're going to have sex with multiple partners. According to a recent survey, the average lifetime number of sexual partners for men and women in the United States is 7.2. Not really sure how that .2 factors in there, but I was an English major for a reason.

Hey, maybe you've had one sexual partner. Maybe you've had 401. IT DOESN'T FUCKING MATTER. During the Victorian era, a woman would be vilified for showing her ankle. At least those days are gone . . . for the most part.

Policing and judging other women for having consensual sexual interests that are different from yours IS NOT OKAY. You're actually not being a good role model or ally to other women if you slut-shame others. You're playing right into the enemy's hands and perpetuating sexism.

There's no shortage of ways that women are judged on the daily. Whether or not someone has had more sex than you or likes sex more than you or likes to have consensual sex with different types of people than you, their fucking isn't your fucking business. There's a double standard at play here, and just like every other type of systemic discrimination, it's all rooted in supremacy.

Infighting among the oppressed is what keeps us oppressed. They want us to battle amongst ourselves and to fight each other for their approval. This is not how we're going to reach equality. Establishing a hierarchy based on sexuality is damaging to all women, and calling another woman out for being sexually empowered is damaging to you and her and all of us.
We can model the exact behavior we want to see in the world. Monitor the language you use for other women, *especially* in front of girls and boys.

Monitor the language you use for yourself. Don't judge yourself or other women for their sexual choices, their clothing, their makeup, or their bodies. Let's just make it really easy: don't judge other women for anything, period. Once we stop fighting with each other and trying to tear each other down, we will become a badass united front. We can become absolutely unstoppable.

Girl, I am really looking forward to that day.

WRITE A THANK-YOU LETTER

There was a period in my career when I had no career. I was in my mid-twenties in Chicago and I couldn't get hired anywhere, no matter what I tried. Then one afternoon, my friend Wynne called me (this was before texting) to tell me that a new TV station airing vintage TV shows was starting in Chicago and I should apply for a job there. She knew that I was obsessed with all things classic TV. The station, WCIU, was looking for someone who could create funny promos for classic TV shows such as *The Munsters*, *Leave It To Beaver*, *That Girl*, and *The Love Boat*. Because I ~~wasted~~ enjoyed seven hours a day watching classic TV reruns as a kid, I was perfectly suited for this job. Before the interview, I wrote a bunch of funny promo scripts based on scenes and soundbites that I had memorized. They thought I was awesome and/or extremely weird, so I got the job. A year later I was writing promos for a national cable TV network, and a year after that I was on staff at NBC.

Many years later, looking back at the trajectory of my career, I realized that my launching point was that job in Chicago, and it was all because one friend was kind enough to call me and give me a tip.

So, out of the blue, I thanked her. I sent her a note and said,

"Everything I have accomplished in my career can be traced back to one moment when you reached out and told me about a job opening. All of the shows I've written and produced, my Emmy Award, all of the ridiculous jingles I've written for TV, the fight I got into with Nell Carter about the size of my feet, my entire TV career can be traced back to that one phone call from you. Thank you!"

Look at your life. There's probably one person somewhere who gently pushed you in a direction you never imagined. A moment, in retrospect, that was gigantic. One person might be behind that moment, and that person deserves to be thanked. Maybe it was a teacher. Maybe a neighbor. Maybe a friend.

Whoever they are, they should be thanked. They'll feel terrific for knowing how they helped someone, and you'll feel terrific for acknowledging them. Everybody wins.

Also, put it in writing. Gratitude of this level deserves a hand-written note.

MAKE GOOD ON YOUR PROMISES

When I was in fourth grade, I told my teacher, Mrs. Virginia Enman, that I hated boys and I would never EVER get married. She laughed and assured me I was mistaken. I was so sure, we made a bet.

The deal was, if I never got married, Mrs. Enman would have to pay me thirty-five cents. But if I ever got married, I'd have to buy her an ice cream sandwich. I remember very clearly writing up the contract, both of us signing it, and Mrs. Enman putting it in the top drawer of her desk.

Twenty-seven years later, a couple of days before my wedding, I tracked down Mrs. Virginia Enman. This is how the call went.

"Hello."
"Hello, is this Virginia Enman?"
"Yes, it is."
"You may not remember me, but I want to let you know that I officially owe you an ice cream sandwich."

A SHORT PAUSE, THEN A FAINT GASP.

"This is Wendy Miller. You're getting married."

Teachers are the greatest.

Look back at your life. Are there lingering agreements that you never honored? Maybe an old argument in which, over time, you've realized that the other person was actually correct? Call that person. Admit when you're wrong. Make good on your promises. Bury the hatchet and close those doors with grace and humility.

Mrs. Enman wouldn't allow me to send her an ice cream sandwich, so I made a donation to a local food pantry in her name instead. Make good on what you say. Be that person. Because, regardless of the argument or the deal, when you make good, you're always the winner.

INTERVIEW AN OLD PERSON

My neighbor is a ninety-four-year-old woman named Sidonia. When she was a girl in Poland, her parents were murdered by Nazis.

Orphaned, hiding in a dirt hole under a building, she was starved, jaundiced and covered with lice. The Nazis eventually found her, shipped her in a cruelly overstuffed freight car to Auschwitz, where her head was shaved, her last belongings were stripped away, and she received a tattoo with the ID A-14821 on her left forearm.

Literally escaping death multiple times, she somehow survived that nightmare and went on to inspire thousands with her miraculous story. Over the years, I've grown very close to her.

Despite enduring unspeakable horrors, she somehow managed to remain positive. One day I asked her how she did it. How did she survive such horrific circumstances?

She said, "When I was in the camp, I noticed a lot of the prisoners working in the kitchen had shoes that were falling apart. So I taught myself how to repair shoes using whatever I could find around the camp. Then I began fixing the kitchen workers' shoes. As a thank-you, sometimes they'd give me an extra piece of bread. That's how I survived."

Every time I'm with Sid, it's like talking to Yoda with a Polish accent. The depths of her knowledge, experience, and perspective are unequaled. The fact that she survived the unimaginable and somehow found her way to America, got married, and created a whole new wonderful life makes all of my first-world problems seem ludicrous.

Talk to old people. Interview them. Play cards with them. Visit them often. Most of them would love to share their wisdom with you, and many have seen and lived through things you could never imagine.

There are endless lessons to learn when you spend time with someone who's lived decades more than you. Plus, they're usually very happy to see you.

TRAVEL BACK IN TIME

What were your favorite things to do as a kid? What were your dreams? What got you really excited? Maybe you loved to dance. Or ride Ferris wheels. Perhaps you loved putting on shows with your friends in the backyard. Or you loved reading your favorite books in a treehouse.

As we grow into adulthood, especially as women, we become more self-conscious and find ourselves exhausted from stress, playing a game rigged against us, and suffering endless microaggressions. Well, a great way to return to the joy of your youth is to put yourself in that headspace. Think back to the time when your worries were microscopic compared to today. Of course, I realize that many readers may have faced serious challenges as kids, but there is an inherent hopefulness, curiosity, and sense of wonder in youth.

Travel back in time, put yourself in that headspace, and write down everything you loved to do when you were a kid. Tap into that joy of creativity you once had, with no fear of judgment.

Write down everything small and big that you remember loving. From playing kickball in your neighbor's front yard to chasing fireflies to drawing or riding your bicycle around the neighborhood without a care in the world.

Now look at that list and figure out how to do some of those things again.

Maybe you can't play kickball in your neighbor's front yard, but might be able to find a local kickball league. If you enjoyed riding your bike as a kid, get on a bicycle now and experience today's world and your amazing life through the eyes of eight-year-old you.

If you loved going to carnivals, find a local one and spend the day enjoying the rides, eating cotton candy and remembering how fun it feels to be free and curious again. This is a great way for you to reconnect with your younger self. Talk to her, encourage her creativity and bravery, and let her know that she's going to grow up to be a total badass.

Kids have an incredible way of looking at life, and over the years we can lose that natural wonder and become jaded and stressed out. Tap into that younger you. That hilarious and weird kid you used to be. Become her again, if only for a day. You might not be able to find a pair of red Toughskins™ jeans, a Marcia Brady poncho, or Dr. Scholl's sandals, but there are all sorts of ways you can recreate and experience some of the happiest moments of your youth.

Only this time, you'll be able to eat all the corndogs and slushies you want, and ain't nobody gonna stop you.

TAKE A WALK

On March 19, 2020, Governor Gavin Newsom issued a stay-at-home order to preserve the public health and safety of California residents. COVID-19 cases were raging out of control, and lives were being lost at a terrifying rate. Well, it turns out that being told I wasn't allowed to go anywhere was the single greatest motivation I ever had to go somewhere.

I'm not a serial rule breaker, quite the contrary. I'm also relatively lazy. But for some reason, starting March 20, 2020, early in the morning, I went for a walk in my neighborhood. A neighborhood I had lived in for seventeen years. Suddenly, I was seeing it through a completely different lens. Like everyone else, my stress level was through the roof. I was laid off from work. I had no idea how I was going to pay my bills. I was terrified that my family or my elderly parents might die from COVID-19. Everyone's fear and stress levels were off the charts. So I started walking.

Full disclosure, I am not an outdoorsy, nature type. I have never even peed outside. I am not rustic. I'm urban. Well . . . technically suburban, but you get my point.

However, when the world went sideways and we were locked in, I busted out. And I walked. At first two miles a day. Then three miles a day. Then four miles a day. Every single morning. Same time. Same exact route.

Within ten months I dropped fifty pounds. Just by walking. And please forgive me if you're one of my friends who occasionally joined me in the morning, but I HATED when anyone walked with me. This became my sacred time. My focus and my healing. MY TIME. I use the time to work out creative problems. To practice gratitude. To understand my stress and my food issues and my fears and break them down with every single step.

Each morning I take the exact route at almost the exact same time of day every day, seven days a week. Walking four miles every single day has changed my body, given me a practice to get centered and express gratitude, cleared my mind, and given me an amazing daily reset, not to mention some well-needed vitamin D.

I lost fifty pounds in only 2,920,000 simple steps.

Get walking and find your own path to feeling great.

TAKE A COMMUNITY COLLEGE CLASS

In 2020, one art history class at Princeton University could set you back almost $5,700. At LA Valley Community College, an art history class would run you about $138. I am not even remotely suggesting that the education you'd get at LA Valley College is comparable to Princeton. Because at LAVC there's a really great taco place right across the street.

Don't be a fucking snob! This isn't about telling people you went to Princeton, 'cause really, nobody fucking cares. This is about finding really fun ways to grow as a person. I don't know about you, but I'd prefer to grow for $138 as opposed to $5,700. Plus, I was politely asked not to return to college, so there's no way I'd ever get into Princeton, anyway.

All over the country are amazing community colleges with really robust course catalogs and tons of options that are extremely affordable and fun. You might even qualify for financial aid. World Music. Sign Language. Religion. Black Studies. Creative Writing. Oceanography. Photography. Anthropology. Personal Finance. There is a world of amazing classes nearby at affordable rates with no entrance essay required!

Plus, scientists agree that continuing education keeps your adult brain stimulated and has long-term cognitive benefits such as increasing memory and confidence, helping you adapt to change, encouraging natural curiosity, and finding new meaning in life.

New meaning in life for $138! I spent more than that on bras last week.

If you want to brush up on ornithology or are thrilled with criminology or can't get enough of lepidopterology, get your ass over to the local community college and sign up for an amazing course. For less than the cost of three dinners, you can enrich your life, exercise your brain, and take college classes entirely for fun.

I used to resent those ancient, thirty-five-year-old "Back To School Ladies" who'd sit in the front row of my classes at American University and be all enthusiastic, always raising their hands and contributing some dumb tidbit about F. Scott Fitzgerald. I hated those bitches. Of course, I also hated college, which might explain why I was politely asked not to return. But now is *your* chance to be one of those Back To School Ladies and get into a heated discourse on the Italian Renaissance. Botticelli for the win!

The bottom line is, there are all sorts of amazing courses out there that can benefit you mentally, professionally, and/or personally, and they're only a few bucks. You don't need to be at Stanford to learn all about the Stanford Prison Experiment. Take some eye-opening classes at your local community college.

If you're lucky, there just might be a great taco place right across the street.

TEST DRIVE YOUR DREAM CAR

I am obsessed with cars. Seriously obsessed. I shop online for them all of the time and dream of owning certain models one day—I'm talking to you, mid-seventies BMW 3.0CSi.

Now, obviously this little adventure doesn't exactly work with vintage cars, unless you're really cute and the person selling it has nothing else better to do. But you know who also really has nothing else better to do? New-car salespeople. They are just sitting around waiting to sell someone worthless fabric protection, worthless window etching, and worthless warranties.

NEVER BUY AN EXTENDED WARRANTY. EVER.

Sometimes for funsies, I will go to a local car dealership and take a model for a test drive. Something really sporty. Something really fancy. Something really indulgent. If you want to be taken seriously, you have to get into the right headspace and dress appropriately. Also, if you're a woman, prepare to be completely ignored and/or condescended to on an epic level. Trust me, I do this activity a lot.

Have you always dreamed of owning a Corvette?

Take one for a test drive. Can't stop staring at the new Porsche 911s? Get behind the wheel and open one up. Enjoy being disappointed by every aspect of a car's fit and finish? There's probably a Saturn for sale somewhere.

Test driving cars doesn't cost you a penny. At least ten times you'll be offered free coffee, and you'll get to hit the road in all sorts of nifty cars. Of course, you'll have to sit next to some rando with slicked-back hair and a flea market silk tie, but that's no worse than riding the subway.

But, if you feel the need for speed . . . or love that new minivan smell, for a fun adventure head over to a car dealership and hit the road. "What's it going to take to get you to buy this car today?" Hmmm, what's it going to take for you to shut the fuck up?

Pro Tip: You will have to show them a valid driver's license, but do not let them hold on to it. Also, DO NOT EVER give them a valid phone number.

Trust me on this.

EAT SOME DAMN DOUGHNUTS

I went to college with a woman who was so afraid of gaining weight that she'd sit in the dining hall, night after night, slowly eating a small salad for dinner while holding one hand on her stomach the entire time. She was truly terrified of getting fat. Eating every meal with a hand on her stomach, hyper vigilant that she was never too full.

Every night before bed, I'd stare in astonishment as she'd purposefully assemble the next day's outfit, deliberately laying out and ironing each article of clothing in advance. Even when she wore boots, she'd make sure that the socks underneath, that no one ever saw, perfectly matched the rest of her ensemble. She was always on some sort of self-imposed lockdown, always, ALWAYS in control.

Over the years we lost touch. But I learned from a mutual friend that my college roommate had been diagnosed with ALS in her early fifties. She spent the last portion of her life in a wheelchair, being fed through a tube and unable to speak. Then she was gone.

I think about the countless meals she unremittingly prevented herself from enjoying. The constant vigilance with zero tolerance for recklessness. No irresponsible acts for the fuck of it. No midnight runs for doughnuts. No crazy road trips to nowhere. Always staying locked down. And now . . . she's gone.

Please. Look at your life. Look at the pleasures you're depriving yourself of. Then, look at what terrifies you most, and then run right into that shit like it's Walmart on Black Friday.

Maybe you're afraid to leave a career you hate. Maybe you're afraid to leave a toxic relationship. Maybe you're not writing that novel.

All of this is fleeting.

You get to decide. You can spend your life on a self-imposed lockdown, or you can choose to do crazy stupid fun shit while giving zero fucks about what anyone else thinks. Go on ridiculous adventures. Take up welding. Build a blanket fort in your living room. Spend a week at a nudist resort. Visit Stonehenge at sunrise. Speed around the entire island of Moorea on a Vespa. Wear mismatched socks. Do every ridiculous thing you can. And when you do go on that midnight doughnut run, savor every single sweet, sticky, wholly irresponsible, cholesterol-soaked bite.

Our time here is short. Enjoy the fuck out of it.

TAKE A BICYCLE TOUR

A friend of very long standing (after a certain age, you really shouldn't use the term "old friend") and I took a girls' trip to Montreal. We wanted to go to Switzerland, but we couldn't work it out. So we went to the Switzerland of North America: Montreal!

No, that's not an actual thing, it's a lie we told ourselves. Now please stop interrupting me!

In all honesty, Montreal is quite beautiful, and it's a great place for women to travel because it's insanely safe. You can walk around late at night without worrying that you'll be jumped. The worst that can happen is you'll get rained on, and even the rain in Canada seems genuinely apologetic. We stayed in a super posh joint, the Hotel St. James on St. Regis Street, or maybe the Hotel St. Regis on St. James Street. I don't remember, and it doesn't really matter. The place was insanely nice, wherever it was.

Before we arrived, we had arranged to take a citywide bicycle tour on our first day there. The tour had great reviews and we thought it would be fun. That morning, when we arrived at the bike shop, we learned that we were the only people who had signed up for the day's tour. So I said to our very cute tour guide, "Let's make this your best day ever. Instead of the usual touristy bullshit places you visit on this thing, take us to *your personal favorite* spots all over town." The guy was overjoyed. Or maybe just Canadian. Both, eh?

Regardless, we hopped on our metric bikes and went on the most awesome tour all over Montreal. His favorite coffeeshop. His favorite stores. His favorite neighborhoods. Because he was gay, all of his favorite places were super fab. Plus, since everyone knew him, we got free stuff everywhere we went. Free food tastes better. We rode up and down hills, past universities, through the business district, in a quaint town square that used to be frequented by turn-of-the-century hookers. We played piano in a park and ate poutine from a trailer. All of the things. It was an absolute blast.

Also, riding around in that crisp and clean Canadian air worked wonders on our jet lag. At the end of the day, we'd covered a ton of miles, saw all sorts of nifty places, ate some weird flat bagels, and made amazing memories.

Plus, we totally learned our way around town, got a ton of exercise, and made a new friend who gave us two cans of legit Canadian maple syrup. Montreal is so much better than Switzerland! Yes, I know I'm lying to myself, please don't remind me.

My point is, there are parts of your city you've probably driven or walked past hundreds of times without knowing their history. Little shops that sell interesting, weird things. Bridges and neighborhoods and back alleys that all tell a story.

Bicycle tours are a great way to get some exercise in and learn the surprising history behind places you zoom right past every single day.

It's also a perfectly awesome activity to do on your own, because you'll either make some friends for a day or be a happy antisocialite doing your own damn thing. Either way, you win!

Read some online reviews and schedule a bike tour for yourself today. Exercise + finding new places + occasional free food = fun!

STRAP ON A TOOLBELT

I seriously love fixing things around my house. Which is surprising, since most of my projects go sideways . . . until they go right. I might have to make three separate trips to the hardware store in one day, but so does everyone else!

It can be frustrating, but I can now walk into almost every room of my house and point out something I installed, repaired, built, or replaced.

There is something so satisfying about improving your own home. Especially if you're a woman. I used to have a really crappy car and every couple of years one of the taillight bulbs would die. I could go to a mechanic and pay them $45 to replace a bulb, but after doing a tiny bit of research, I discovered it was only a couple of screws that were easily accessible from inside the hatch. So I went to a local auto parts store, bought a replacement bulb for a couple bucks, snapped open the housing, and with a few basic tools replaced the bulb in minutes. MINUTES!! I saved at least $40 every time, but the satisfaction of knowing I did it myself was worth a fortune.

Home improvement projects may seem absolutely daunting, but have you ever actually chatted with a contractor? These people are not Neil deGrasse Tyson. They just have a bunch of tools and have done things enough times that they feel they can charge you $100 to install some shelves.

Well, let me tell you, sister, EVERY SINGLE STEP you need to know about basic home improvement projects can be found in a poorly shot online video. From resetting a stuck garbage disposal to installing a light fixture to setting a toilet or putting some shelves in your closet, YOU CAN FUCKING DO THIS!!! And you should! Plus, power tools are fun, and you might actually find someone working in the hardware store who is totally helpful.

I'm joking, of course.

The bottom line is, it's a radical feminist concept to take back all of the bullshit that men have claimed as their domains. Watch a few videos, buy a circular saw and some good hand tools (not any of that overpriced pink shit), and start fixing stuff in your house!

There is absolutely no way you cannot do this. It might not turn out perfect, but that's totally okay. Perfection is the enemy of finished. Put some holes in your wall. You can repair them. Replace your bathroom faucets yourself. Install tile flooring in your entryway. It's time for some Home Empowerment!

Everything you need to know is available online. Once you tackle your first project, you'll be addicted. In a good way. Being able to fix things in your home or car is a radical concept, and you are a radical fixing badass.

So strap on a tool belt and fix your own shit!

CLEAR OUT YOUR CRAP!

I was at a retreat that may or may not have involved sacred, psychedelic plant medicine. My life-changing download was the following:

> *"If you want abundance,*
> *the first thing you have to do*
> *is get rid of everything."*

Since then, I have been on a quest to get rid of all of the crap in my life, and in doing so my life has improved in a myriad of ways.

The things all around you make noise. Clutter makes a lot of noise. Clearing out the clutter in your space can clear your head and help you focus much more efficiently. Now, before you start blaming yourself for owning fifty pairs of shoes you'll never wear, you should know that each of us is forced to run the gauntlet of a multi-billion-dollar, highly focused and nefarious lie telling all of us that MORE STUFF is the answer to all of our problems. On average, we see five thousand advertisements A DAY.

Each advertisement basically invents problems you never knew you had, and then suggests that various products (Order Today!) will fix your life/body/health/beauty/house/transportation/places to poop, etc. That's a lot. On some level, we all want to show off our stuff. It's human nature. Unfortunately, human nature is dumb as fuck. As they say . . .

> *"Too many people spend money they haven't earned,*
> *to buy things they don't need,*
> *to impress people that they don't like."*

Please buy what I am selling you right now. More Stuff will not make you happy. More Stuff will not make you feel accomplished and sexy. More Stuff will not solve all of your problems. More Stuff is an asshole.

Here are some benefits to not buying More Stuff: You will have more money to spend on better things such as amazing experiences, self-improvement, real estate, or extra copies of this book. Your house will not be cluttered with crap. Your space will be easier to clean because there will be fewer things to dust/hide when your parents come over. Buying Less Stuff is better for the environment. The less we consume, the fewer boxes we need, the less fuel is used to transport it, and fewer natural resources are destroyed.

But I need More Stuff!!!

No. You actually don't.

Americans spend more than $20 billion a year on off-site storage for their excess stuff. That is a lot of extra stuff!

Despite what you've been told by the fine people who sell More Stuff, having more stuff will not make you feel better or happier.

Maybe for a minute or two, but then the treadmill starts right up all over again. That happiness is fleeting, and the more you have, the less happy you'll be with what you have, which will only make you think you need more. Which you don't.

My sister Mindi is taking this to a whole new level by practicing something called Swedish Death Cleaning. Not the most aspirational name, to be sure, but the concept was popularized by a book called *The Gentle Art of Swedish Death Cleaning: How to Free Yourself and Your Family From a Lifetime of Clutter* by Margareta Magnusson. This practice is about getting rid of the crap you've accumulated over your lifetime. Crap you no longer need. That way, after you die, you're not burdening your family with a basement, attic, and storage rooms full of your crap. Not an inherently sad process, it's basically identical to what I'm suggesting, only it has better branding.

I am not suggesting the end result should be a completely barren apartment that looks as if you've just been burglarized. What I am suggesting is for you to examine the things that are actually stressing you out without your knowledge. You are never going to touch that stupid fondue set in the back of your pantry. You don't need fifty pairs of socks. That closet full of used toddler toys is almost as annoying as an actual toddler. There are items all around you that are mocking you.

But there are many people out there who can really use them. You probably have a lot of clothes you're never going to wear that you can donate to others. If you're super fancy, you can also sell your items and use the cash for better things, such as family experiences or more copies of this book for your friends. Since that enlightening night for me, I have been on a quest to get rid of most of my crap. I've donated tons of clothes, furniture, toys, shoes, posters, PEZ dispensers, kitchen items, dishes I'll never use—all sorts of things have been passed on to others who can benefit from them.

I've never regretted getting rid of anything, and I feel grateful to be fortunate enough to share my stuff with other folks. My house is less cluttered, and someone else gets a fondue set they'll actually use.

Everybody wins!

If you truly want to simplify your life and quiet the noise around you, focus on what's truly meaningful. Help others while you also help yourself.

Get rid of More Stuff.

CLEAN OUT YOUR BOX

Now that we've had the important conversation about getting rid of the clutter lying around your house, it's time to get rid of the massive amount of clutter in your email inbox.

Obviously, the email in your inbox isn't stacking up in your personal space, but it can be a source of anxiety and stress. Are you really going back to read those emails you've been hanging on to for ten years? No. You are not.

There are certain services and apps you can use to help you clean out your inbox and unsubscribe from as many junky emails as possible. You can also go analog on your digital hoard and just start deleting. It's so damn rewarding. If you feel guilty trashing all of those emails with Aunt Misty's cat photos, an easy way to lighten the load is to create folders.

You can make huge changes by creating folders of an entire year. All of your old emails from 2017 will be right there in a separate folder and out of your inbox. You can create folders from specific senders: Aunt Misty, your credit cards, social clubs you belong to —all can be easily sorted into their own folders.

Separate by medical records, school, or bids for your new bathroom remodel. You can create custom folders that will make your content easily sortable and still accessible, without cluttering up your inbox.

It's kind of a Zen practice. Don't think you need to do it all at once. Just pick one person, one theme, or one year and start moving the clutter out of your inbox and into folders. Eventually you'll feel lighter and way more organized. Plus, you'll get rid of tons of e-crap you've been hoarding for no reason whatsoever.

If it's been sitting in your inbox unread for years, there's a good chance you don't need it.

So delete it.

PITCH A TENT

I'm a cancer survivor. A pretty gnarly cancer. And to make matters even more bizarre, two years after being diagnosed with cancer I was in a horrible motorcycle accident where I suffered a traumatic brain injury and was in a coma. It was literally a coin flip whether I would live or die. Luckily the coin landed on Wendy Gets To Live!

It's experiences like these that really shape a person. When you're given TWO NEW LEASES ON LIFE you hopefully learn not to take anything for granted, not to dwell on fear, and to have much more perspective in your life. And in many ways, I do have that. I rarely allow myself to be in shitty situations. I do not suffer fools, and I have what I consider to be a strong understanding of the capriciousness of life.

But surviving two brushes with death in two years didn't completely embolden me. That's a lot of PTSD to work through, and even though it's been thirty-plus years since I almost died twice, I do have the occasional emotional aftershock. Now I recognize it and work through it. It all takes a while.

Yet with all of my enlightenment, I still let a few things hold power over me. And one of those things was going camping.

I'm not what you'd call a rugged individual. My idea of roughing it is low thread count sheets. I have never peed outside. I'd never slept outside. The only extended time I spend outside is either playing golf or enduring a double header at Wrigley Field. As I mentioned earlier, I'm not outdoorsy. And I proudly made that MY THING, to the point where I basically bragged about how inflexible I am.

Then one day, I began to deeply evaluate my rigidity. Why was I so terrified of sleeping outdoors? How many maniacs really run rampant in the suburbs searching for campers to murder in their backyards? I mean, I don't watch the local news, so if it is going down, I haven't heard a thing.

Fuck it! I decided to sleep outside!

I put up a tent in my backyard. I had purchased the tent years earlier so our kid could pretend she and her friends were camping in the living room for a slumber party. We're not an outdoorsy family, in case you haven't figured that out yet.

I packed the tent in my backyard full of blankets, lights, snacks, water, more blankets, several pillows, my sleeping bag, my kid's sleeping bag, a phone, a power bank, and a spare pair of glasses and decided to rough it!

Twenty feet from my kitchen door.

Now, some of you might be thinking, "Big fucking deal. I've slept on a rocky riverbank in the freezing rain, covered in leeches." Well, you were clearly on *Naked and Afraid*, and whatever anyone else does has nothing whatsoever to do with me anyway.

Jerry Lewis supposedly wore a brand-new pair of socks every single day. Does that mean I should? Nope.

Comparison is the thief of joy. I'm pretty sure Jerry Lewis never thought about me when he was putting on his new socks, so why the fuck should I be thinking about him?

And anyone else who mocked me because their version of camping was way more authentic and rustic than mine also does not even remotely matter.

Your fears are your fears. Whatever you choose to do has nothing whatsoever to do with me, or anyone else, for that matter.

So around 9:45 p.m., I crawled into my tent with my friend Tara, who decided to join me for the night. I tried to get as comfortable as possible. I shut my eyes. Then, a menacing sound rang out.

SFX: Genuine Spooky Owl

Tara assured me the noise was only an owl, but I was pretty sure it was a maniac with a rusty hook looking for middle-aged women to murder in their backyard tents. She didn't seem that worried, so I decided this was probably my best shot at facing my fear. After all, I didn't hear any John Carpenter music. So I pulled the sleeping bag tight around my head, wedged myself into the corner of the tent, and shut my eyes, hoping for the best.

No one thought I would make it longer than an hour.

Nine hours later, I woke up in the morning. Totally un-murdered. But also no longer afraid of spending the night outdoors. Like everything else, I faced it, I did it, and just like that, I took away all of its power. Another fear bit the dust.

Just like that. I mean, my back was killing me for a day or two, but hey, that's the price you pay when you're a rustic outdoorsy type like me.

Now, maybe a few of you are thinking, "So what? It's not scary to sleep in your backyard. This is lame." I kindly reply, "It doesn't matter what anyone thinks about me. That's none of my business. Period."

Now if you'll excuse me, I have to pack a few bags. 'Cause I'm going camping...in my backyard.

LEARN TAROT

I'm interested in all ideas as long as they're ethical, not trying to convert me to some religion, and not aiming to stick me with something worthless.

I'm also interested in things that are mystical and otherworldly, except for Dungeons and Dragons. And kombucha. I think it's fascinating to try to communicate with other realms, and I love the excitement of gaining insight into the past or future.

Tarot is a type of fortunetelling or divination using a specific deck of cards, and its early uses date back thousands of years. I truly believe that some people have intuitive gifts. I've occasionally had very clear psychic premonitions that came true, but it's not something I can rely on or summon with any regularity. I do know to listen to them when they flash in because they can be astoundingly accurate. If only I was told to buy Bitcoin in 2009...

If you are so inclined and want to be the center of your social circle, you can learn how to read tarot cards. There are various online courses available, and you might be able to find a high-level practitioner who will take you under their wing and teach you how to read the cards.

Some people believe that you should be given your first deck of tarot cards, but many experts say that's not necessarily true. Shop around and see which deck speaks to you. Many readers recommend beginning with the Rider-Waite tarot deck. Originally published in 1909, it's considered the most popular deck for tarot card reading. It's also the one used in most books, teaching websites, and video tutorials.

Don't put pressure on yourself. Look at this as a way to learn something unique that might help people. Mastering new skills is great for your self-confidence, and being able to give a friend a reading can be very exciting. So go ahead and teach yourself tarot.

I see a lot of enjoyment in your future.

WRITE A SONG

Over the years I've composed hundreds of jingles for NBC, *The Wayne Brady Show*, and my podcast *Sex Ed The Musical*. I love writing songs, and just picking up a ukulele or sitting at the piano to create music is very fun for me.

I think it can be fun for you, too.

First of all, don't psych yourself out. Can't play an instrument? No problem. Can't read music? No problem. Got a cruddy voice? Me too! Can't sing in front of other people? No problem.

None of those roadblocks should stop you.

And don't put any pressure on yourself to create a masterpiece. This is your song, so you can't possibly get it wrong. Maybe make it your own personal "get psyched" song or a melody that helps your wind down at night and brings you comfort. You can create your own beautiful music. Give yourself permission and space to play with a tune and create something special just for you.

You have a voice. Let it sing your own magical song.

GET MOVING

I don't know who came up with the quote, "Dance Like No One Is Watching," but I really wish they'd shut up already. In fact, I think you're much better off if you dance as if someone IS watching. Specifically, a dance teacher. Otherwise, why are you paying them?

My friend Myrna dragged me to a Zumba class one day. I was in the back of the room because I'm a back-of-the-room kind of dancer. At one point during the class, a woman in front of me turned around and asked if she was blocking my view of the teacher. When I asked her why, she said because I seemed to have so much difficulty learning the steps. She assumed that she was blocking my view. First of all, Zumba is hard! Secondly, it's not your fault that I'm a crummy dancer, but thanks for asking.

Total lack of dance skills aside, I was having a really fun time. I've actually taken hours and hours of tap, jazz, and ballet classes. Was I good at any of them? Absolutely. Not.

Does that even matter? Nope.

There are all sorts of dance classes you can take that do not require a partner. Ballet, tap, jazz, Bollywood, hip hop, country line dancing, Irish line dancing, Samba, Zumba . . .

and the best part is you don't even have to leave your house. Multiple studios offer dance classes online. Some are even for free.

Soul Train Line of Only One, for the win!

Dance is a great way to relieve stress, improve your cardiovascular health, help your balance, increase strength and stamina, boost cognitive performance, elevate your self-esteem, and improve your mood. Plus, you get to wear leg warmers!

Dude! Leg warmers!

So go ahead and sign up for a dance class and dance like someone IS watching!

You!

PET PROJECT

If you love animals but can't have your own pets, consider volunteering at a local rescue or animal shelter. Volunteering helps with the common good, orphaned pets have a lot of love to give, and tons of places can really use your help. Just know that it's not all sitting in a pile of kittens and playing with them for hours at a time. A lot of real and sometimes messy and hard physical work needs to get done. From cleaning cages, filling food and water bowls, walking dogs, and socializing furry friends, to bookkeeping, creating adoption posts online, and transporting pets in need of shelter, there's always something you can do to help.

Also, KITTENS!!!

If you have a camera, you can help take adoption photos. You can assist at adoption events, create fundraisers, or even read to lonely shelter pets.

Also, KITTENS!!!

Call local rescues, shelters, or the Humane Society to see how you can volunteer. Each place has different needs and requirements. Be sure you're clear with your own physical limitations as well. These places are busy and they really need consistency, so make sure that you can commit to a regular volunteer schedule. Each place is different.

Most of these shelters and rescues could not exist without volunteers, but you will get so much more out of helping pets in need. It's scientifically proven that spending time with animals helps lower your stress levels and blood pressure. By volunteering, you get to help a cause that you care about. You really are making a difference in an animal's life. You stay active and get to spend time outside with furry new friends.

Also, KITTENS!!!

TELL YOURSELF TO SHUT UP

In September 1996, I was ten months into a super cushy staff gig at Game Show Network. Days were spent writing and producing jingles and silly promos for vintage game shows such as *Password*, *The Dating Game*, and *What's My Line*. On paper, this was my dream job.

One night, I was invited to my first big-time "celebrity party" in the Hollywood Hills. I remember standing there, happily chatting with some famous-adjacent folks about a goofy new Kitty Carlisle jingle I had just produced. Comedian Janeane Garofalo, who was standing a few feet away, reeled around and yelled, "If I have to hear your fucking Kitty Carlisle story one more time, I'm going to throw up all over the fucking floor!"

She's nice.

The truth is, I had grown as bored with making vintage game show promos as Janeane Garofalo was with eavesdropping on my story.

As luck would have it, a few weeks later, I learned that NBC was searching for a staff writer and producer to join an innovative new department that produced breakthrough bonus content running on a split screen during the end credits for *Seinfeld*, *ER*, *Mad About You*, etc. NBC2000 created original comedy material, TV show parodies, trivia questions, and all sorts of fun content designed to retain viewers during the end credits and sweep them right into the next show. I sent them my demo reel. A few weeks later, NBC made me a three-month trial offer. I quit my Job For Life® at Game Show Network and headed to beautiful downtown Burbank.

My first few days at NBC were spent writing jokes for Goat Boy and trying not to make waves. I had utilized a similar "try not to get fired" strategy a few years earlier at *a very famous talk show* but sadly, as you're going to read in a minute, that did not net the desired result.

Here's why: If you have a big opportunity somewhere, the very LAST thing you want to do is play it safe, keep your head down, or try to fade in.

You need to take big swings and let everybody know you're there. Think about it. There's a reason you don't hold your arms to your side and quietly whisper, "Excuse me . . ." when you're drowning. You scream as loud as you're able and thrash your arms to literally make a splash. A chance-of-a-lifetime opportunity is the same. You need to MAKE A SPLASH.

Or you're dead.

I was dying at NBC. My three-month trial was quickly winding down and there was no splash. I hadn't even made a puddle. Then one day, we were told they needed a promo for an upcoming episode of *Frasier* where Niles decides to make his big move on a newly single Daphne.

With nothing actually smart to suggest, I blurted out the first dumb idea that fell into my head. Something completely ridiculous and obscure. "Let's do a parody of the old commercial for the board game Mystery Date," I stupidly suggested.

Honestly, I have absolutely no idea where this goofy idea came from. But instead of playing it safe, not making waves, and suppressing my stupidity, I threw it out there. I really had nothing to lose at that point. My boss thought for a moment and shrugged, "M'okay."

For some reason unknown to me, the producers of *Frasier* also liked my stupid idea, so we shot a frame-by-frame parody of the obscure, vintage TV commercial with the *Frasier* cast. The very ridiculous idea that fell out of my face, the stupid idea whispered to me by the Curator of the Museum of Obscure Vintage TV References that exists in my head, the stupid idea that anyone else would immediately suppress, got me hired on staff at NBC. The courage to be an idiot (and the fact that I passed the mandatory drug test) was all it took.

I thrived, stupidly, at NBC for years. I was eventually promoted to Director of Special Projects, and I wrote, produced, directed, and edited thousands of pieces of content years before that word was even used. I learned everything I know about marketing, I made friends for life, and I did, without a doubt, some of the greatest work of my career.

Until I got bored and quit.

That's a story for another time. My point is, if you ever find yourself drowning, please don't play it safe. Splash as much as possible. Take chances. As Mark Twain said, "Why not go out on a limb? That's where all the fruit is."

So how can you access all of your inner stupidity? It's quite simple, once you learn the trick.

There's a voice in your head. Okay, if you're a creative person, there are probably several very loud and interesting voices in your head. But for the moment, let's focus on that one very prominent voice that prevents you from making bad decisions. Most of the time that voice is doing you a big favor.

- *Don't walk down that dangerous alley at night.*
- *Don't use a giant knife to help you reach a box of precious porcelain cups perched on a high shelf.*
- *Don't buy an English car.*

This voice saves you from guaranteed disaster. Unfortunately, this voice is also a huge, power-mad asshole. This voice prevents you from accessing your true creative genius. This voice doesn't want you to be groovy. This voice demands that you always play it safe. This voice is a dick. Okay, yes, this voice occasionally saves your life, and I suppose that can be helpful. Unfortunately, it also has a really strong side hustle suppressing your awesome and stupid ideas. This voice always wants you to play it safe. Well, I got some news for you and this voice: Your "dumbest" ideas are probably your best ideas.

Meanwhile, playing it safe is a one-way ticket to nowhere.

Every unique, silly, and risky idea that magically drops into your brain is forced to run a gauntlet of self-doubt, judgment, fear, and completely irrelevant comparisons before you'll even consider it. Meanwhile, your safe and totally obvious, crappy ideas are immediately escorted right to the front of the line, like Cher at LAX. The entire system is completely backwards.

No offense, Cher.

What if we can somehow invert the entire Idea Regulating Process (IRP™) inside your head?!!? After all, it's your head, so you can do whatever you want with it, right? On board? Here's how to do it.

First thing, give that voice a name. Something you'll remember. My judgmental voice is named Roberta. She's awful. Next, thank that voice for repeatedly saving your life. "Thank you, Roberta. I'd be dead without you." Now that she's feeling appreciated, quickly tell her to take a well-earned break for a couple of hours. "Roberta, thank you again for your service. Preventing me from inserting a wet screwdriver into that live electrical outlet last week was super smart. You totally saved my ass. Again! You so rock. In fact, you have done such a bang-up job of keeping me alive that I'm gonna send you on a little vacation as a reward. That's right, Roberta. I'm going to be working on a silly creative project now that has absolutely nothing to do with you, so if you wouldn't mind, please step away and enjoy your time off while I access my stupid, creative ideas. I promise you, I'll check in before doing anything that might get me killed, arrested, or slapped. But right now, go on a super sweet vacation while I'm working on something else. Thanks, Roberta! Byeeeee!!"

It's that simple.

Send Roberta away for a while. She'll be fine. If you start to freak out from all of your newfound creative freedom, you can always temporarily reinstate Roberta. Maybe while you go to a public bathroom or have to cut a bagel. You can put Roberta back in charge. Briefly. But when you want full access to your creativity with no judgment, tell Roberta to scram. I promise you she won't get angry. Okay, she might get angry. She's a manipulative power freak, after all. She may put up a big fight and tell you that she always knows better, blah, blah, blah. But here's the thing . . . she doesn't.

Roberta doesn't know better. She's not remotely creative. She hates crazy ideas. She's the finance department, the legal department, and a power-mad mall cop all rolled into one. Roberta is a professional buzzkill who wants to stop you from accessing your most ridiculous ideas because she's afraid you're going to be judged and get hurt. She's afraid you're going to be laughed at and get hurt. She's afraid everyone is going to find out that you're a total fraud and that your ideas are worthless and that the entire world is way more creative and talented than you. Roberta continually undermines your creativity because she's afraid it's going to hurt you.

Roberta is wrong.

What Roberta doesn't realize is that you'll be fine if you take big swings. People are thinking of you a lot less frequently than you imagine. People have their own crap to worry about, so they're not sitting around wondering why you could DARE to suggest such ridiculous ideas.

I've been on both sides of this table. I've been the goofball pitching stupid ideas and I've been the tense executive clutching a tiny water bottle on the other side of the table, silently hoping and praying that SOMEONE, ANYONE comes up with a great idea.

People aren't trying to crush you; they're rooting for you. They need you to solve their problems. They need you to write that great book. They need you to design beautiful wrapping paper. They're sitting there hoping and praying that you have a really awesome, gigantic, and stupid idea for them. What they're not doing is sitting there hoping you only have super safe and obvious ideas. I promise you this: Safe, obvious, and derivative ideas are like subway tiles. They're everywhere. Big, stupid, brave ideas that no one else has but you? That's something special.

Which is precisely why you politely have to tell Roberta to fuck off for a bit so you can move your ridiculous ideas to the front of the line. Remember: You can always pull back on a huge, stupid idea, but there's not a lot you can do with beige.

So here's your exercise for the day. Go to your favorite work spot. Get comfy. Grab a beverage and a tasty snack. Now give your own Roberta a name, thank them for their service, and then ask them, kindly yet authoritatively, to go away for thirty minutes. Just thirty minutes. Once they're gone, spend those thirty minutes generating whatever stupid ideas you've been afraid to bring forward. Painting, poetry, design, knitting, screenwriting, photography, a business plan, sculpture . . . whatever it is, spend thirty minutes with your Roberta on ice and see what kind of gigantic and stupid ideas you have in there. Don't edit yourself, don't look back, just generate stupidity like a runaway train for thirty minutes. Then stop.

Now look at what you have in front of you. Behold what you have created. You have thirty minutes of completely judgment-free, unregulated creativity. While you're reviewing it, Roberta may try to chime in and tell you your ideas are crap, but this isn't her department. Send her back to her soulless office. You're busy.

Look at what you've created. It may be brilliant. It may be a gigantic pile of stupidity. I hope, for your sake, it's both. Try this exercise with more and more frequency until it becomes second nature. Do it over and over again until it becomes creative muscle memory. Once you can quickly get rid of your Roberta and access your great wealth of stupidity without judgment, you'll be off to the races. You will be a brave and ridiculous, carefree idea machine.

Seriously, forget about Roberta. She'll be fine. She has plenty of other things to worry about.

HELP OTHER WOMEN

Every Tuesday morning, I would play golf with a client who was a big TV executive. Whenever any of his shots came up short he'd yell out, "Hit the ball, Mary!" as if to insult himself by using a woman's name. I would take enormous pleasure whenever I outdrove him because 1) I can be very competitive, and 2) He was being a total sexist prick with that bullshit comment even though he probably didn't even realize it.

This is an example of unconscious bias, and sometimes women are guilty of it as well. It could be cultural or generational or completely accidental. You might drive into a car repair shop and see a female mechanic and for whatever reason assume she's the least skilled one there. Little do you realize that most male mechanics don't know what they're doing either, but that's an entirely different conversation. Another problem is that men have created a world that systematically prevents women from accessing decision-making and power. When we do ascend to leadership positions, we have to deal with a double-bind in which we're either regarded as competent or likable, but rarely both.

I've worked with several alpha dudes. Guys who've used intimidation and bullying to run their departments, and everyone thought that was leadership. Yet during my annual employee review at one company, I was told I was being "too bossy" and "mean to the people who were not as smart as me." Too bossy in the department of which I was the actual boss? And "mean" to people not as smart as me? Can you imagine a man getting the same critique? It's unthinkable.

When men are forceful it's called leadership. Women? We're called bossy and shrill. Even women in high-level leadership roles are expected to be likable in order to accommodate male feelings. Then if we're seen as too soft because we've been forced to accommodate men's feelings, we're not considered strong leaders. We can't win.

Convenient.

At one TV network, I was reprimanded by a male V.P. for "sitting defensively in meetings" because I held my arms folded against my chest. When I explained it was because the male President of the department would stare at my tits during meetings, he walked that one back.

Scarcity of access is deliberate. When it's perceived that there's only one seat at the table for a woman, many men delight in watching us fight each other for it. Or fight each other over anything. It's exciting and potentially arousing to them. Plus, I think in many ways some guys love when women fight each other because they are imagining the women fighting over who gets to have sex with them.

Before I continue, I respectfully insist that we never use the term "cat fight" ever again. The term is inherently sexist and offensive. Even to cats. First of all, there's no sexist term for a fight between men, it's just called a fight.

Secondly, the term dehumanizes us, literally. It's belittling and turns any altercation between women into a cartoonish sporting event. Men have pitted us against each other for millennia because that serves them very well. But not only do we need to be taken more seriously as humans, we need to do whatever we can to support each other, amplify each other, build our own damn tables, and populate them with leadership that is truly reflective of our values and society as a whole.

Plus, working with women has proven benefits. Not only are the companies with little to no female leadership depriving themselves of a greater diversity of viewpoints, but a Harvard School of Public Health study found that companies with the highest number of female directors on their boards had fewer overconfident male CEOs making reckless decisions, which yielded higher benefits for shareholders.

More women = More $$$

Here are just a few things you can do to support other women:

Hire Other Women – When you are staffing a new project or even looking for a new plumber, you can't keep going to the same well and expect different water. Cast a wider net. Examine the race and gender breakdown of your candidates. Deliberately search for underrepresented people and ask for diverse referrals from others. Make a commitment to uplift, mentor, give access to, and support BIPOC and queer women. Use your privilege to help underrepresented women whenever you can.

> "I raise up my voice—not so that I can shout,
> but so that those without a voice can be heard…
> We cannot all succeed when half of us are held back."
> —*Malala Yousafzai*

Encourage Other Women – This goes back to the scarcity issue. If you're an aspiring novelist and another woman sells a book, her success has nothing to do with you. It's not a zero-sum game. Support and encourage women who are putting themselves out there. Use your network to amplify another woman's work. Celebrate each other's work. Be of service. Give access. Help your friends reach their dreams however you can. Sometimes it's as simple as a phone call or a note of support. Be there for your friends. Lift your friends. Be the Oprah of your friend group. Extra credit if you have a cream-colored cashmere turtleneck and a bunch of cocker spaniels at your feet.

Be Authentic – In this Pinterest/Instagram world, there's so much pressure on us to appear perfect at everything. So many people seem to have art directors in their living rooms. Not me. I am the queen of Pinterest fails. My IG photos aren't framed perfectly. I never use filters. My cake balls are a disaster. My bedroom is a mess most of the time, and you know what? That's fine. Celebrate your quirks. Give your friends permission to be human, and model behaviors of self-acceptance. Share your struggles. Laugh at your fails. Celebrate your lopsided cake balls.

Perfection is not attainable, and it's also not fun. Don't trade your authenticity for approval. You'll never respect the person you've become.

Make Your Compliments Matter – It's one thing to say, "You look pretty today." Totally nice and innocuous. Maybe next time, try saying, "I love how you make so many amazing choices in life." Which one would you rather hear? I'm not suggesting that you script compliments in advance. I'm suggesting that you can really uplift someone by not focusing on physical attributes or superficial things. Focus on the things that really matter, and let your friends know that you appreciate them.

Be *That* Friend – Keep extra tampons and pads in your desk, even if you don't use them. Always carry a tweezer with you. Tell someone when there's food in their teeth. Show up. Listen and don't offer suggestions unless they're requested. Keep chocolate in your house. Share your belongings with no expectations of getting them back. Pick up the check. Be that friend.

Whether it's in middle school or middle management, we've all dealt with Queen Bee Syndrome where some women in authority treat the women below them like garbage. The biggest bully I ever had was a female vice president at NBC who had it in for me from day one. She didn't even bother to get to know me before hating me. One afternoon, she quite aggressively tried to throw me under the bus in front of my bosses. Tired of her bullshit, I went up to her office, fists clenched, to beat the shit out of her. Look, you and I are friends now, I'm just being honest here. Anyway, as I stood across from her, cautiously calling her out on her bullshit while plotting which of her two faces to pummel first, she acted as if it never happened. Total gaslighting bullshit. I endured years of this treatment from her, and everyone in management knew it.

Many, many years later, we happened to be at the same NBC reunion party. She was predictably standing among all of her former male bosses, and I was predictably as far from her as possible. Finally, she walked up to me and said, "I just want you to know I'm really sorry about how I treated you at NBC." Completely caught off guard, I replied, "Oh, that's okay, don't worry about it."

Do I regret not punching her in the face that afternoon at NBC? Sometimes. But what I regret much more is immediately letting her off the hook. She totally caught me off guard when she apologized, and it was an accommodating reflex that I think many women have. "Oh, don't worry, that's okay." Fuck that!

I should have asked her, right then and there, why she was such a monster. Why she made the lives of so many other women at the company miserable. Why she was such a raging piece of shit. But I was so stunned, I just let her off the hook.

Former U.S. Ambassador to the United Nations Madeleine Albright famously said, "There's a special place in hell for women who don't help each other." Accountability is critical, and we must stop tearing each other down. We have to lift each other up. We have to be there for ourselves, and for each other. We have to.

Period.

LEARN FROM OTHER PEOPLE'S MISTAKES

Not too long ago, a friend asked me, "What was your worst day ever?" I thought about it for a moment. Maybe I should pick the day when I was told I had cancer and my mother turned to me and said, "Oh, good, maybe you'll lose some weight." Nope, that's just too darn obvious.

Maybe I should pick two years after my cancer diagnosis, when, after reaching an important cancer milestone, I got in a near-fatal motorcycle accident and spent several days in a coma. No, that's actually kind of funny in its irony and I'm here to talk about it, so who gives a fuck.

Let's skip all the near-fatal cancer/head injury shit. The truth is, I pretty much look at everything through the prism of television, so I will share the lesson of my worst day ever, in television. After all, television is far more interesting than anything that ever happens in a hospital. Unless it's a television show set in a hospital, and then very few facts apply.

I was in Chicago freelancing as an associate producer for the most popular talk show in the history of the world.

My duties included researching show topics, finding guests, field producing, coming up with show ideas (remember the Hot Dog Diet, anyone?), and assisting my assigned producers in any way I could. It was a really fun place to work if you like stress-based colitis. Anyway, we were doing an episode called "Would You Risk Your Life For A Stranger?" and during the taping I was hanging out in the booth trying not to get fired. That's my usual motivation.

The taping was in between acts, and the executive producer, a frighteningly powerful woman, was running through the teleprompter to see who the next guest was. As I stood in the back of the booth, I thought I noticed a mistake. I was pretty sure the name on the teleprompter was not the next guest, but actually someone who was scheduled to appear much later in the show.

I nervously took a deep breath and with a very weak voice from the back of the booth said, "Um, excuse me, Frighteningly Powerful Woman, um, I think that's, um, the wrong name in the prompter."

Frighteningly Powerful Woman reeled around and screamed, "Get the producer in here now!!!!!"

Well, as one who knows how to take an order, I ran out of the booth and down the hall into the studio where I saw the producer standing. I ran right up to her and without pause said, "I think there's a mistake in the script and Frighteningly Powerful Woman needs to see you in the booth right now!"

Then my limited vision expanded full screen and I realized that the producer was deep in conversation with the host of the show and I had interrupted them. Badly. Nobody did that. Like, ever.

The producer reeled around and glared at me while the host looked at me in that "Who the fuck is this person interrupting me during a break in the show that I own in the studio that I own on the city block that I own?"

It was at that point I wanted to die. For real. Forget all those actual brushes with death that I previously had, at that moment I was hoping I really would die and vaporize right on the spot. In that glare-filled split second I realized I should have waited until they had finished talking and then oh-so-casually pulled the producer aside to tell her that Frighteningly Powerful Woman wanted to see her in the booth. But I didn't.

I just didn't.

The producer excused herself from the most beloved talk show host in the history of mankind and headed to the booth. I walked fifteen paces behind her and then waited in the hallway, still trying not to get fired. Moments later the producer emerged from the booth, and with tears streaming down her face she screamed, "Don't you ever do that to me again!!!"

With that, she walked back into the studio and I limped upstairs to pack up the few things I had on my desk. At that point I absolutely knew that I would never be invited back to that show again.

For years I dwelled on this moment. How could I have been so stupid? How could I have been so inappropriate? I was going to be persona non grata with them forever. Plus, I had a sworn enemy who would go out of her way to destroy me at any chance she got. That might sound a bit petty and dramatic, but until you've worked in daytime TV, you have no idea what kind of a snake pit it can really be.

Flash forward many years later. I was executive producing several TV shows for a network ironically co-owned by the talk show host herself. One afternoon, I happened upon the phone number for the Frighteningly Powerful Woman, who had started a new gig at NBC, and gave her a call. We chatted for a while and then I told her that she was part of my worst professional mistake ever. When I recounted the story, she said, "Well, didn't I tell you to go out there and get the producer right away?"

I said, "Yes, you did."

She then asked, "Was the name in the teleprompter really wrong?"

"Yes," I replied, "The name was actually wrong and it had to be changed."

Frighteningly Powerful Woman took a moment and then explained, "What you did was not a mistake at all. If the teleprompter was wrong and the host read it that way, we'd have to go back and reshoot the segment, which is a massive ordeal, and the host would have been very, very unhappy. Whether the producer knew it or not, you actually saved her ass."

With that I took a deep sigh and released years and years of guilt and shame. I finally realized that on what I thought was my worst day ever, I saved that crying producer's ass. **That's right, I actually risked my life to save a stranger.**

But I bet she still wants to kill me.

Instead of dwelling on your mistakes and replaying them over and over and over in your head until they get more powerful and terrifying, learn from them and move the fuck on.

Yes, I screwed up. Everyone does at some point. The real question is, did I learn an important lesson from that screw up and now I'm a smarter person?

Yes.

Also, and I can't stress this enough, you'd be surprised how infrequently everyone is thinking about you. Yes, you're at the center of your own thoughts but I assure you, you're not at the center of everyone else's thoughts. I mean, okay, we're all marginally interesting but people are fucking busy. Get over yourself. There's an excellent chance nobody is thinking about you.

Like, at all.

Trust me, that's exactly how you want it.

AFTERWORD

My goal for this book is to help you simplify your life, empower you to become a Stealth Superfreak, and inspire you to become the best possible version of yourself. On the surface, this book is supposed to be about how to enjoy a happy and healthy relationship with someone else. But at its core, this book is about *loving yourself*.

Because *you* come first.

In a rare case, I'm not speaking sexually. Although, that's also true sexually. But right now, I'm talking about the concept of making *yourself* a priority. Self-care is a term that's been bandied about a lot, but what does it really mean?

As women, we have a difficult time putting ourselves first. We're concerned about our partner's needs or our children. Worried that if we do put ourselves first, other people will see us as somehow greedy or self-centered. We've been ~~brainwashed~~ socialized to be responsible for everyone else's feelings and needs at the expense of our own. I'd say that's an awfully convenient setup for everyone else. Well, I have a theory about this, and it might be difficult for some to grasp, but I say, FUCK THAT, TOO!

This isn't a zero-sum game. By taking care of yourself, you're not choosing to abandon your loved ones. It just means you are making your health and wellbeing a priority, which means you'll be better able to help others as well. There's a reason they ask you to put the mask on yourself first on an airplane. When you take care of yourself first, you're better positioned to be of service to others.

Not taking care of yourself, not addressing your physical or mental health needs, working too many hours, and not getting enough rest or exercise or fun can have significant consequences. But by establishing and then following a self-care routine, you can reduce anxiety, depression, exhaustion, and anger. There's a direct correlation between self-care and reducing the risk of stroke, heart disease, and cancer.

So what can you do?

Remain Socially Connected. Spend time with your friends. Your support network is there for you. Set regular times to be with your people. They heart you.

Get Healthy. Exercise can seem like a chore, but if you focus on the positive aspects of it instead of unrealistic physical goals based on bullshit beauty traps and social constructs, you will get so much more out of it. Daily exercise produces stress-relieving hormones and improves your general health. Try to eat healthier foods. Trust me, there are times when you will see me in the Jack in the Box drive-thru getting a taco or four. I'm not going to pretend I'm all kale and tofu up in here. But in general, I am mindful about what I eat and how it makes me feel. This is not about restrictions or hitting some target weight based on aggressively photoshopped images. This is about making the best choices for yourself. By eating more unprocessed foods, you can lower your risk for chronic illness and stabilize your blood sugar, energy, and mood. Get some sleep.

It's a radical idea to go to bed early, but giving your body a chance to recharge and rest is critical for your mental and physical health. Meditation, stretching, and a daily practice of gratitude can all make a huge difference in your health and wellbeing.

Set Boundaries. I am all about boundaries. I boundary like a motherfucker. My boundaries are protected by razor wire. I will not put up with some shit. But this took me a long time to learn and put into practice. Of course, there have been some people who got all bent out of shape about my boundaries. Those are people who would benefit from me having none. Setting boundaries empowers you and protects you. Boundaries can also vary with different people. You might be happy to drive one friend to the airport, while another person who constantly asks you for favors will get a hard no. That's fine. Your boundaries, just like consent, can change and evolve, but you must establish them first. Boundaries are your bestie.

Treat Yourself. Take a nap in the middle of the day if you want to. No need to explain yourself. Get a mani/pedi if that makes you feel groovy. Watch your favorite movie three times in a row by yourself. Buy a new outfit. Take a knitting class. Try a flotation tank. Lie in the sun and read a trashy novel. Have ice cream for dinner. You don't want to look back at your life and realize that you wasted most of it because you were afraid of being your authentic self, or worried about what other people think.

Are total strangers, neighbors, relatives, or people you barely care about the ones who get to set the direction of your life? For years I was afraid to share my own story because I didn't want to be judged by a particular pair of super catty moms at my kid's school. I actually allowed two horrible people who mean absolutely nothing to me, to derail my life's work. It finally dawned on me that their opinion of me doesn't matter. Only one opinion of me matters. Mine.

My goal is to inspire you to live the best, most fulfilling, happy, sexy, smart, and fun life possible. We're not going to be here for very long, and the last thing you want to do is die with a bunch of regrets.

Live your life. Love your life. Love your body, and love others around you. Laugh. Help other women, BIPOC, queer and underrepresented folks whenever possible. Do stupid things. Be grateful. Follow through on your promises. Don't worry about what others think of you, and don't worry about what other people are doing. That has nothing to do with you. Focus on taking care of yourself, and having all of the consensual sexual pleasure you desire.

That way when it's your time to go, you'll know you lived life to the fullest on your own terms, helped others less fortunate, enjoyed a ton of fun and adventure, and had the happy and healthy relationship you've always fucking wanted.

That's the point of all of this.

THANK YOU

If you've enjoyed reading this book I would be very grateful if you leave a review (it can be as short as you like) on the book's Amazon page.

Also, please feel free to share the book with all of your friends and all of the people who used to be your friends. I sincerely thank you for reading and supporting my work.

Your pal,

Wendy

ACKNOWLEDGMENTS

I could not have finished this book without the help of several incredibly generous, smart and clearly underemployed friends.

Thank you to the Happiness Mastermind—Kelly Edwards, Myrna Everett, Jackie MacDougall, and Mindi Miller—who inspire me, call me on my bullshit, and push me way the hell outside of my comfort zone to get some real work done.

I owe an enormous debt of gratitude to my favorite Canadian and Sexologist, Dr. Jessica O'Reilly, eh? A special heart-opening thank you to my life-changing guidance from Sharon Lee. I would not be anywhere near where I am today without the enduring support and endless wisdom of Elizabeth Ury.

I also must thank smartypants Ilyce Glink for always taking my panic-stricken calls, even when she was busy with actual paying clients.

Thank you to Nikki Kessler for keeping me laser-focused on intent. A massive hug to my son, the doctor, Martin Vitorino who teaches me about gender, identity and bravery every single day.

Thank you to Pixie Marineau for her pixelated magic.

Thank you to "New Jersey Gary" Rudoren, for endlessly championing my work.

Mark Guncheon, Johnny "LaRue" Ryan, Frances Callier and Arthur Vibert, I am grateful for your very generous advice.

Thank you to my imaginary best friend Brené Brown for giving me the courage to be authentic and vulnerable in my work.

Thank you to Dr. Anthony Fauci for 2021.

Finally, I must thank my fifth-grade teacher, Miss Kovic, for never once believing in me. You'll never know how much you inspired me to prove you wrong, over and over again.

SEX ED THE MUSICAL

What listeners and experts are saying about *Sex Ed The Musical*...

"This podcast is genius."
— Dr. Sherry A. Ross, Ob/Gyn, Author, and Host of of the
series, *Lady Parts*

"Thank you for creating a space to talk about sex in ways that
are supportive, affirming, educational and fun."

"As a woman who at 56 just recently rediscovered her libido or
as I like to say had "her pilot light re-lit" in a surprising way I
can't wait to hear more of this podcast. Outstanding!"

Featuring enlightening and fun interviews with leading experts
in the world of sex and women's health, bestselling authors,
comedians and incredible people living fun and adventurous sex
lives. Be sure to listen to and follow my podcast,
Sex Ed The Musical.

Because, YOU come first.

SexEdTheMusical.com

ABOUT THE AUTHOR

Wendy Miller is an ACS Certified Sexologist, Relationship Expert, an Emmy Award-winning TV producer and comedy writer, and the creator/host of the hit podcast, *Sex Ed The Musical*.

Wendy has been a speaker at Sexual Health Expo, has hosted numerous, sold-out, advanced sexual technique seminars, has appeared alongside top sex educators and physicians on multiple sex panels and has produced and supervised hundreds of hours of sex-positive, premium adult programming.

She has written, produced and/or directed for NBC, VH1, ABC Family, Paramount, AMC, *The Oprah Show*, *The Tonight Show*, *The Wayne Brady Show*, Telepictures, Buena Vista, TV Land, Lifetime, Oxygen, and Playboy TV.

Wendy is a proud member of the Producers Guild of America, and Women of Sex Tech. She lives in Los Angeles, is happily married to a handsome actor you have seen on TV, and is the mother of an epic badass teenage girl.

For media inquiries or just to say hello, go ahead and reach out to Wendy through her website: thewendymiller.com

COPYRIGHT

Made in the USA
Columbia, SC
14 March 2022